Tim ...
Professor of Accounting in Information Systems
Illinois State University

ESSENTIAL
dBASE IV
(VERSION 1.1)

Wadsworth Publishing Company
Belmont, California
A Division of Wadsworth, Inc.

Computer Science Editor: Frank Ruggirello
Editorial Assistant: Rhonda Gray
Production: Bookman Productions
Interior and Cover Design: Vargas/Williams/Design
Compositor: Graphic Typesetting Service, Los Angeles
Printer: Malloy Lithographing, Inc.

 2 3 4 5 6 7 8 9 10---96 95 94 93 92

ISBN 0-534-18721-8

CONTENTS

PREFACE

Purpose

This *Software Essentials* book and its associated software training materials teach software competency. These materials are designed for both majors and non-majors in a quarter or semester course that uses the microcomputer as the primary vehicle for introducing students to problem solving. As typically expected in this type of course, there are no prerequisites.

Approach

Students acquire software competency by completing a set of software-training chapters that focus on current releases of various major software packages. To achieve that competency, each software package is presented in a separate booklet emphasizing hands-on problem solving. Carefully prepared, hands-on tutorials are provided within each chapter. Closely related end-of-chapter exercises reinforce the tutorial learning and expand the student's mastery over a broader range of applications.

Software packages covered in this series include

- DOS 3.3 and 5.0.
- WordPerfect 5.0 and 5.1.
- Lotus 1-2-3 (2.2 and 2.3).
- Quattro Pro 3.0.
- dBASE III Plus.
- dBASE IV (1.1).
- Paradox 3.5.
- Windows 3.1.

Improvements in Software Instruction

I have always made the greatest possible effort to make hands-on instruction direct and meaningful. For this series in *Software Essentials*, the hands-on passages have been extensively reviewed and revised to make the booklets in the series more effective for the teacher and learning easier for the beginning student. Important changes include the following:

- **Self-Contained modules** Each software module is self-contained, with its own front matter, chapter numbering, glossary, and command summary.
- **Expanded Hands-On learning** The number of hands-on exercises has been increased dramatically. Particularly, the number of shorter exercises has been increased.
- **Hints/Hazards Boxes** Many Hints/Hazards boxes inform students about the tricks they can use and potential traps they may encounter when using a particular software tool.
- **Keyboard Icons** Keyboard icons appear frequently in headings and tables. These icons help the student identify and remember specific keystrokes.

Working in a Hands-On Environment

Software Essentials and its allied materials work best in a habnds-on environment. The step-by-step exercises make most sense when an individual is sitting at computer and can immediately see the results of his or her actions. A symbol such as the one shown in the margin indicates hands-on material.

Each software package covered in this series is treated in enough detail to satisfy the requirements of a computer novice. However, each software booklet assumes that the software has already been configured for the student's use. If a package has not been configured for a specific machine, refer to the documentation for that package.

Hardware Requirements for Hands-On Software

An IBM PC or compatible computer with two disk drives and 320K of memory is required for most tools in this series. Note that you need 512K and a hard disk to run dBASE IV. You will also need a color monitor/graphics adapter board to properly display Lotus 1-2-3 graphics on the screen. A printer (with graphics capabilities if you wish to print Lotus graphs) is also required for printing documents, reports, graphs, and worksheets.

The hard disk (fixed disk) has resulted in many changes in the way computer concepts and use are taught in the classroom. During the past few years, the prices of hard disk technology have plummeted. Because this technology is now affordable for most colleges and universities, this text includes instructions for running software from a fixed disk.

Learning Aids and Sample Files

Exercises are provided at the end of each chapter to give students quick feedback on their progress. Besides the written exercises, hands-on computer exercises are included at the end of the software chapters to provide feedback through challenging applications of material covered in the chapter. A number of sample diskette files—including sample worksheets, text files, and database files—have been provided for use with text lessons and exercises.

ESSENTIAL

dBASE IV

(VERSION 1.1)

INTRODUCTION
TO DATABASE
AND dBASE IV

CHAPTER OBJECTIVES

After completing this chapter, you should be able to:

- **List some of the basic concepts of database**
- **Plan a file**
- **List the limitations of dBASE IV**
- **Use the dBASE IV Command Center**
- **Know the parts of a dBASE IV screen**
- **Use the dBASE menu options**
- **Issue commands to dBASE**
- **Create dBASE files**
- **Add and edit data**
- **Use some elementary dBASE commands**

The concept behind a *database* is simple. A database is like a filing cabinet. Just as a filing cabinet stores information, so does the database. Just as the folders in the cabinet are arranged in some useful order, so are the records in a database. Searching the database for certain information is like searching in the cabinet. As you can change the order of the folders in the cabinet to suit your convenience, you can also change the order of things in a database.

TERMINOLOGY

A **database** is a set of information related to some specific application. In the context of dBASE, database is synonymous with *file*.

A **record** is a unit within the database. Each record in a database contains related information, such as the details of a single business transaction or a single customer's name and address.

A **field** is a smaller unit within a record. In a customer record, for instance, one field might contain the customer's last name, another his or her street address.

Information from one or more fields is used to define *keys,* which are used to order, identify, and retrieve the records in the database. Several keys are commonly used. The **primary key** is the unique identifier for a particular record, most often a unique record number. When a database is in primary key order, record number 5 occupies the fifth position in the database. A **secondary key** can also be defined by information from one or more other fields within the database. This key is used to arrange the database in some other order. For instance, a user might create a secondary key–containing space for a Social Security number field in order to put a file of employee records in order by that number.

The **structure** of a database is a set of instructions regarding the arrangement of information within each record, the type of characters (numeric or alphanumeric) used to store each field, and the number of characters required by each field. Once structured, the database can be managed, and the computer can be instructed to do such things as adding new records, changing existing records, sorting and arranging records into a new order, searching for and retrieving specific types of records, printing data, and deleting data.

Designing Fields   There are two very important things to remember when designing the fields of a database. First, fields should isolate those bits of data that you may need to use as keys to sort and rearrange records. Second, whereas humans can often identify separate bits of information within a field, computers generally cannot. For instance, consider the following four lines from a customer address file:

Alfred A. Conant
2645 W. Hartford
Moosejaw, IL 61703
(309) 367-8934

How many fields should it take to store these lines in a record? It is possible to store the customer's name in one field. However, it is impossible for the computer to sort records by last names because it doesn't know that Alfred is a first name and Conant a last name. Nor, for instance, can the computer readily tell an address from a telephone number. Thus, designers and users of databases must take care to lay out fields and enter data in rigid, predictable patterns. The computer can therefore process information in the database solely on the basis of what field it is in, without any understanding of the meaning of the data. In practice, the above customer information requires eight fields:

First Name	Address	ZIP
Middle Initial	City	Phone
Last Name	State	

The name is divided into three fields so that records can be sorted by last name and the first name can be used independently of the middle initial. Divisions in the address line let you rearrange records within the database by city, state, or ZIP code.

Well-designed records provide great flexibility when you choose secondary keys. With the preceding fields, for instance, to produce a report in order by customer names, you could create a key based on first and last names. By changing the keys to last name and city or state, you could produce another report in order by customer name and location.

INTRODUCTION TO dBASE IV

The dBASE package is the best-selling relational database package on the market. The current version of dBASE (dBASE IV, release 1.1) evolved from **dBASE II**. Ashton-Tate originally developed dBASE II for 8-bit microcomputers that used the CP/M operating system. When IBM introduced the IBM PC, Ashton-Tate revised dBASE to run on the PC/MS DOS operating systems.

When Ashton-Tate first thought of developing dBASE II, it envisioned a software package for the narrow market of systems developers rather than for the general public. The dBASE II developers assumed that users would have certain programming and systems development skills not usually found among the general public. The resulting package was not user-friendly.

This became a problem when the package became tremendously popular and began to sell to users who were unskilled with computers and programming. To overcome this and to take advantage of the power of the IBM 16-bit microprocessor, Ashton-Tate introduced the **dBASE III** package. This new package provided an Assist feature for low-level users and allowed many more fields per record.

When users demanded an even friendlier program with even more power, Ashton-Tate responded by introducing **dBASE III Plus**. This offered the ability to network and a full-featured user interface that operates by menu selections and thereby avoided making the user enter instructions from a dot prompt. A user could concentrate on solving a problem rather than on learning dBASE language.

With **dBASE IV**, Ashton-Tate has further increased the power of dBASE. The maximum number of fields has been increased from 128 to 255. It has increased the power of the user interface and now refers to that as the Control Center. It has added a compiler to provide for faster execution of dBASE programs. It has also added a System Query Language (SQL) feature that has become standard within the information systems arena.

LIMITATIONS OF dBASE IV

Anyone who wants to use the full version of dBASE IV should be aware of the following limitations: (1) It requires an IBM PC or compatible computer with a fixed disk with at least 3.5MB of available storage; (2) the system should have 512K of RAM; (3) it should hold 1 billion records; (4) the maximum record size is 4,000 characters and 255 fields; (5) a character field can have up to 254 positions; (6) no more than 10 database files can be open at one time; and only 10 indexes can be specified as active for a file at one time. Most applications are not affected by these limitations.

dBASE IV MODES

The dBASE IV package provides you with three different modes. The **CONTROL CENTER mode** is an easy-to-use menu-driven interface that lets you issue commands without an in-depth understanding of dBASE. **COMMAND mode** requires some understanding of dBASE because instructions are entered at the **dot prompt** (.) and Help menus are not displayed for most commands. **PROGRAM mode** (also referred to as BATCH mode), lets you store instructions in a program file and execute all of them with one command.

STARTING dBASE IV

Because dBASE IV is so large, it can only be run on a computer containing a fixed disk. Starting dBASE requires you to first boot your computer (if it is currently off) and then enter the date and time, if you want to have this information in the directory (provided that your computer does not have this clock/calendar feature). You now use the DOS Change Directory (CD) command to activate the directory containing the dBASE program files. If, for instance, your dBASE IV directory is named DBASE, enter the command CD\DBASE. After you have activated the directory, start dBASE by entering the command DBASE at the DOS prompt.

THE CONTROL CENTER

Once you have started dBASE IV, the copyright screen appears (Figure 1.1). This screen shows who purchased the package, the company at which this person works, the serial number of the package, and conditions of the copyright agreement. This screen disappears after a few seconds or when you press Enter, and the Control Center is displayed (Figure 1.2).

You may have a copy of dBASE that has the Control Center menu display inhibited via settings in the CONFIG.DB file. In such a case, you will be placed at the dot prompt of dBASE, and a screen like that depicted in Figure 1.3 appears. This screen is composed of two parts: the dot prompt and the **status bar**. In such a situation, reactivating the Control Center menu requires you to enter the Assist command and then press Enter. The Control Center menu depicted in Figure 1.2 now appears on your screen.

Parts of the Control Center Menu   The Control Center contains a series of menus that allow access to many of dBASE's commands and features.

Menu Bar (F10)   The top line of the Control Center, the **menu bar**, contains the names of three menus and a clock. Activate this menu by pressing the F10 function key. Once F10 is pressed, the submenu for the Catalog option appears on the screen in the form of a pull-down menu (Figure 1.4). When a pull-down menu appears on a dBASE screen, you can select options in one of two ways: (1) by moving the menu bar/pointer using the Up or Down Arrow keys

Figure 1.1

The copyright screen of dBASE IV

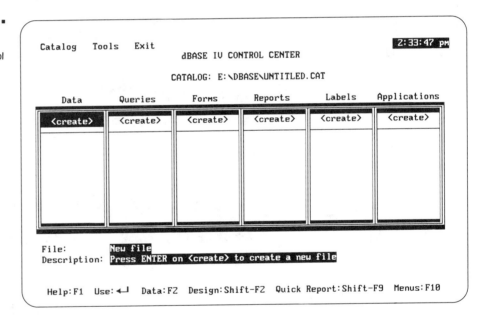

```
                                                    Ashton-Tate
        This software is licensed to:               Ashton-Tate
                                                    Ashton-Tate
              Tim Duffy                              Ashton-Tate
        Wadsworth Publishing Co.                   Ashton-Tate
             000931194-27                         Ashton-Tate
                                                 Ashton-Tate

        Copyright (c) 1986, 1988, 1990.  Ashton-Tate Corporation.  All
        Rights Reserved. dBASE, dBASE IV and Ashton-Tate are registered
        trademarks of Ashton-Tate Corporation.
        You may use the software and  printed  materials in  the dBASE IV
        package under  the terms of  the Software License  Agreement;
        please  read it.   In summary,  Ashton-Tate grants you a paid-up,
        non-transferable,  personal license  to  use  dBASE  IV on  one
        computer  work  station.   You do not become  the owner  of the
        package nor do  you have  the  right  to  copy  (except permitted
        backups  of  the  software)  or  alter  the  software  or printed
        materials.   You  are legally accountable for  any violation of the
        License Agreement and copyright, trademark, or trade secret law.


        Press ⏎ to assent to the License Agreement and begin dBASE IV
```

Figure 1.2

The dBASE IV screen with the Control Center menu activated

```
 Catalog   Tools   Exit                                        2:33:47 pm
                              dBASE IV CONTROL CENTER

                          CATALOG: E:\DBASE\UNTITLED.CAT

       Data       Queries      Forms      Reports      Labels    Applications

    <create>    <create>    <create>    <create>    <create>    <create>










   File:        New file
   Description: Press ENTER on <create> to create a new file


   Help:F1  Use:⏎  Data:F2  Design:Shift-F2  Quick Report:Shift-F9  Menus:F10
```

Figure 1.3

The dBASE dot prompt screen

```
 .
 Command                                                          Num
```

to highlight the desired option from the menu and then executing that option by pressing Enter or (2) by entering the first character of the menu option. You can only position the cursor to an option that is in high-intensity video on the screen. An option that appears in low intensity is not available for execution and cannot be reached by using cursor positioning commands or by entering the first character of that menu option.

●●●●●●●●●●●●●●●●●●●●●

Figure 1.4

The Catalog submenu from the menu bar activated by pressing F10

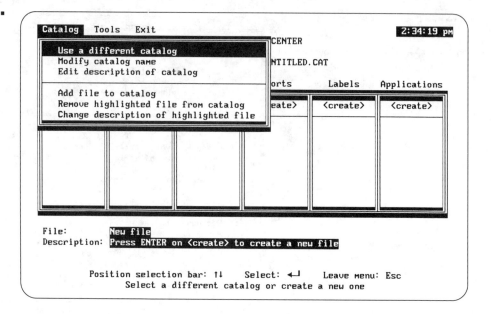

●●●●●●●●●●●●●●●●●●●●●

Figure 1.5

The pop-up menu that appears after selecting the Add file to cat-alog option

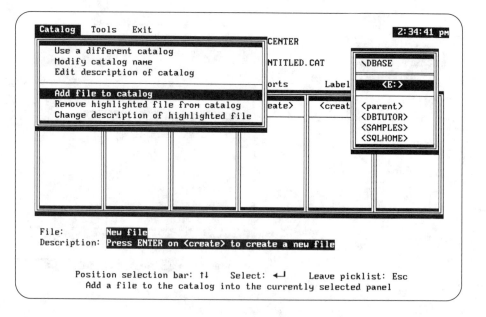

You can also, once a menu is activated, move horizontally from one menu option to another across the menu bar by pressing a Right or Left Arrow key. When you are moving horizontally, you cannot issue the first character of a desired menu option.

Once a submenu option is selected, pop-up menu boxes may appear on the screen. For instance, if you select the option Add file to catalog, the pop-up menu like that depicted in Figure 1.5 appears on the screen. Users frequently make mistakes using menu-driven packages and suddenly find themselves in a menu that is completely unexpected. In such a situation, press Esc to clear the pop-up menu and return to the prior menu.

When pressing Esc, be careful about issuing the command once you have been returned to the Control Center menu. If you press Esc from the Control

Figure 1.6

The pop-up menu that places you at dot prompt level by pressing Esc at the Control Center

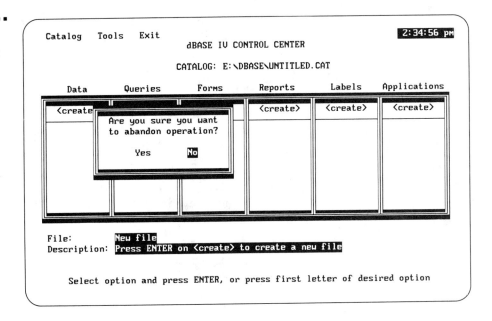

Center, dBASE displays a message like that depicted in Figure 1.6. If you mistakenly respond Yes to this prompt, you are taken to the dot prompt of dBASE. To return to dBASE requires that you issue the Assist command.

Catalog The **Catalog** entry indicates the set of related files on which you are working. For example, you can have a set of files that are related to a Christmas-card mailing list or a set of files related to a payroll or inventory application. The Catalog entry includes data about the path of the files to let you know exactly where on disk the files are located.

The concept of a dBASE catalog lets you categorize together all files that are logically related to a specific application. By dealing with these logically related sets or groupings of files, dBASE only displays the files necessary for a given application. Files that are used for other applications do not appear on the screen, thus avoiding confusion about which files are used for a given application.

Panels The **Panels** portion contains the six types of files that can be built using the Control Center. For example, the Data entry shows the names of the database files in the current catalog. You can access other entries such as the Forms, Reports, or Labels by pressing the Right or Left Arrow keys. The Tab key can also move the cursor to the right, and the Shift + Tab key combination can move the cursor to the left. Any panel can show up to 200 different filenames. The following are the various files for the panels:

- *Data* stores information about applications, people, activities, and the like.
- *Queries* stores information about how data within a file is to be manipulated.
- *Forms* stores specially created screens for entering or viewing data.
- *Reports* contains specifications for headings, totals, and data order used for generating reports from database files.

- *Labels* contains instructions for formatting and printing labels.
- *Applications* stores programs (sets of detailed instructions) that manipulate data.

File Information   The two lines marked F i l e : and D e s c r i p t i o n : toward the bottom of the screen contain **file information** about the filename and a description of the file marked by the cursor.

Navigation Line   The **navigation line** shows which keys are currently activated for issuing dBASE commands to the Control Center. The F10 key is specified for activating the entries contained in the menu bar.

Message Line   The **message line** contains more information about options in the Control Center menus. Most often, the message line further explains a menu option that has been highlighted in a menu box.

THE HELP FACILITY (F1 OR .HELP)

Help is available by highlighting any item in a Control Center menu or any submenu and then pressing F1. For instance, if you want help on the Data panel command, press F1 while that option is highlighted, and the screen displays a description of that command (Figure 1.7). Once you have read the Help screen, press Esc to return to dBASE. Another way to get help is by selecting Help in a pop-up menu (Figure 1.8). This type of pop-up menu appears when you commit an error in entering a command at the dot prompt. Highlighting Help and pressing Enter displays the Help screen for that command (Figure 1.9).

You may also want general help from the dot prompt but are not exactly certain about the command for which help is needed. In such a case, entering the **Help command** generates a Help menu like that depicted in Figure 1.10.

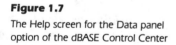

Figure 1.7

The Help screen for the Data panel option of the dBASE Control Center

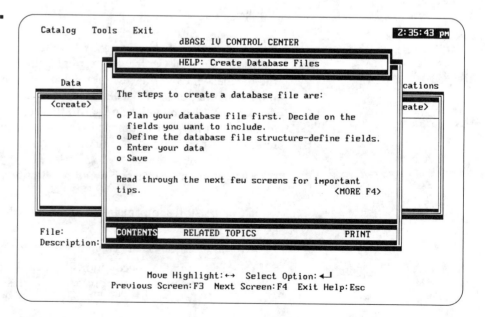

Figure 1.8

The general Help menu that can be obtained from the dot prompt level of dBASE

Figure 1.9

The Help screen for the Store command entered from the dot prompt

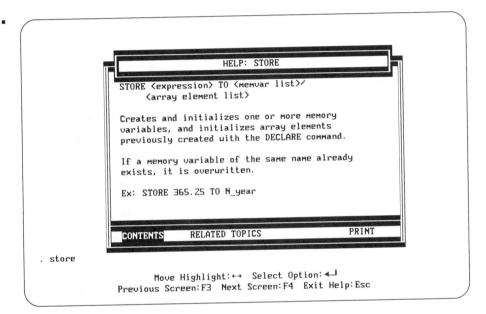

Figure 1.10

The Help menu for the single Help command entered from the dot prompt

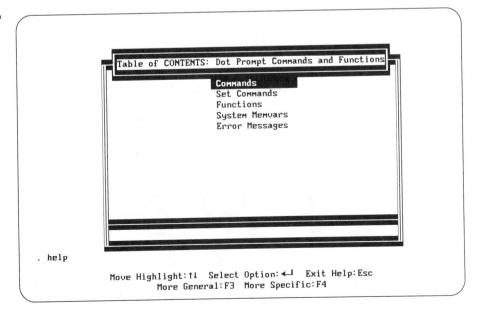

- -

Figure 1.11

The alphabetic listing of commands
for the Help command option

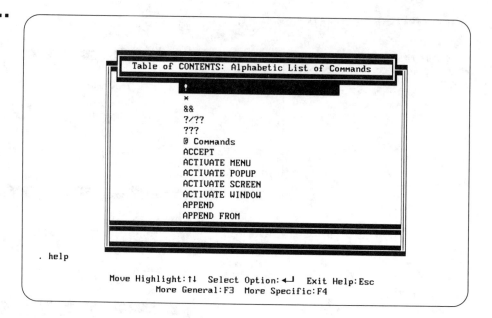

. help

- -

Figure 1.12

An example of the Related Topics
option for the Report command

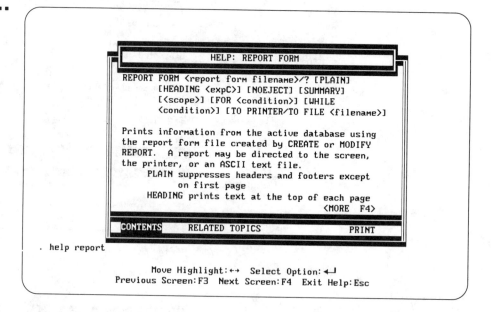

. help report

Once this command is issued, select the option about which you want more
information, press Enter, and select from the menu of options that are displayed to the screen. Figure 1.11 shows options that appear when the Commands entry is selected. You can also get help by entering the Help command
followed by a specific command. For example, Help Report results in a Help
screen concerning the Report command.

When you are in the various Help screens, the navigation line contains
prompts about how to move from one screen to the next. Press F3 for the
previous screen, F4 for the next screen, or Esc to exit. Notice also that each
Help screen contains a Contents, Related Topics, and Print (Figure 1.9). The
Contents entry returns you to the alphabetic table of contents, the Related
Topics entry shows you the various commands that are similar to this command (Figure 1.12), the Backup option (when visible) functions in the same
manner as F3, and Print sends the contents of the Help screen to the printer.

LEAVING dBASE IV (F10 + EXIT OR .QUIT)

At the end of a dBASE session, you must properly exit to DOS using either the `Quit to DOS` option in the Exit submenu or by using the **Quit command** at the dot prompt. If a file has had records added to it and is not closed properly, the end-of-file marker will be misplaced, and records may be lost. To quit from the Control Center requires the following commands:

F10   Invokes the menu bar.

Exit   Selects the Exit option of the menu bar by highlighting.

Quit to DOS   Selects `Quit to DOS` by highlighting.

Enter   Executes the command.

To quit from the dot prompt, enter the Quit command and press Enter. Whichever method you choose displays a message and the DOS prompt:

```
*** END RUN   dBASE IV
C>
```

....

COMMUNICATING WITH dBASE IV

This section presents the CONTROL CENTER (menu-driven) and COMMAND (dot prompt) modes of dBASE IV. It also introduces some dBASE commands: Create, Use, Append, List, and Edit.

FROM CONTROL CENTER TO COMMAND MODE

The Control Center is an excellent tool for learning dBASE because it is menu-driven and does not require programming knowledge. For these reasons, we emphasize it in this and the following chapters.

Use the Control Center to learn commands. Once the commands and their proper sequence are familiar, start trying the COMMAND mode. In the long run, COMMAND mode is quicker because you do not have to view several menus before completing a command nor return control to a previous menu before proceeding, as sometimes happens with the Control Center.

At the computer, start dBASE IV as instructed. Because the Control Center is the typical default, the Control Center menu, which lists your initial options, appears.

dBASE Sentence Rules   When you use a series of menus to issue a command to dBASE, regard the series as a sentence. The Control Center forces you to issue commands in the correct grammatical order.

```
COMMAND   SCOPE   NOUN   CONDITION
```

Command tells dBASE what action to perform. **Scope** limits the range of the command, determining whether all or only a part of the file is to be affected. **Noun** is the object—a file, field, or variable—on which the command will act. **Condition** specifies the fields or files to be acted on using relational ($< > =$) or logical (and, or, not) operators. A dBASE sentence need not have all four parts; it may consist of the Command part alone. But if it has other parts, they will come in the above order.

The Control Center constructs sentences in the correct order. Once you are familiar with this order, switch to the more sophisticated COMMAND mode and type such sentences yourself. In using COMMAND mode, remember that you must always sequence your instructions in this order: Command, Scope, Noun, Condition.

To switch from the Control Center to COMMAND mode, press Esc once or twice and respond Yes to the pop-up menu query. This will cause the dot prompt (.) to appear. The dot (actually a period) is the dBASE COMMAND mode prompt and indicates that dBASE is waiting for you to enter a command. After each command, press Enter to execute the command. To return to the Control Center, type Assist at the dot prompt and press Enter.

 ## SETTING THE DEFAULT DRIVE

Unless told otherwise, dBASE assumes that data files are on the same disk as the dBASE program files (this may have been changed for your system). If you want to save files to a diskette, issue the following commands to change the default drive. Begin from the Control Center.

F10   Activates the menu bar.

Tools   Selects the Tools option from the menu bar by highlighting.

DOS utilities   Selects the DOS utilities option from the Tools submenu by highlighting.

Enter   Executes the command.

F10   Activates the menu bar.

Set default drive:directory   Selects Set default drive: directory.

Enter   Executes the command.

Type A: Names the drive and, if necessary, the directory where files are to be saved.

Enter   Executes the command.

F10   Activates the menu bar.

Exit   Selects Exit by highlighting.

Enter   Returns you to the Control Center.

CREATING AND USING A CATALOG

As mentioned previously, a catalog is a dBASE convention that allows dBASE to track all files that are related to a specific application. For example, all files that are related to a payroll application are stored in a catalog called PAYROLL, and all files that are related to a personnel application are stored in a catalog called PERSONNL. A catalog for an application lets you more efficiently track only those files that you use for a specific data-handling task.

When dBASE first starts using a disk device, it places all .DBF files in an untitled catalog and displays that catalog in the Control Center (Figure 1.13). Unless told otherwise, any files that are created are placed in this untitled catalog. To make handling and tracking files easier in using this text, the text examples will be placed in a catalog called CUSTOMER. You will be instructed to create other catalogs and place files in them for use in performing the end-of-chapter exercises.

Figure 1.13

The Control Center with the UNTI-TLED.CAT active

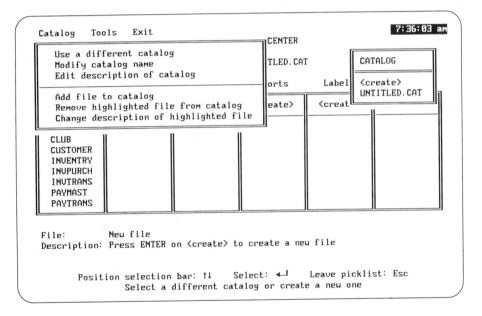

Creating and Activating the CUSTOMER Catalog   The following commands create the CUSTOMER catalog, activate that catalog, and then place a number of files in that catalog (. Set CATALOG TO filename). Start at the Control Center:

F10   Activates the menu bar.

Use a different catalog   Selects Use a different catalog by highlighting. (It should automatically be highlighted.)

Enter   Executes the command. The screen displays a CATALOG box with the names of existing catalogs (Figure 1.14).

<create>   Selects the < create > command by highlighting.

Figure 1.14

The Catalog menu box for activating a catalog

• •

Figure 1.15

The CUSTOMER catalog

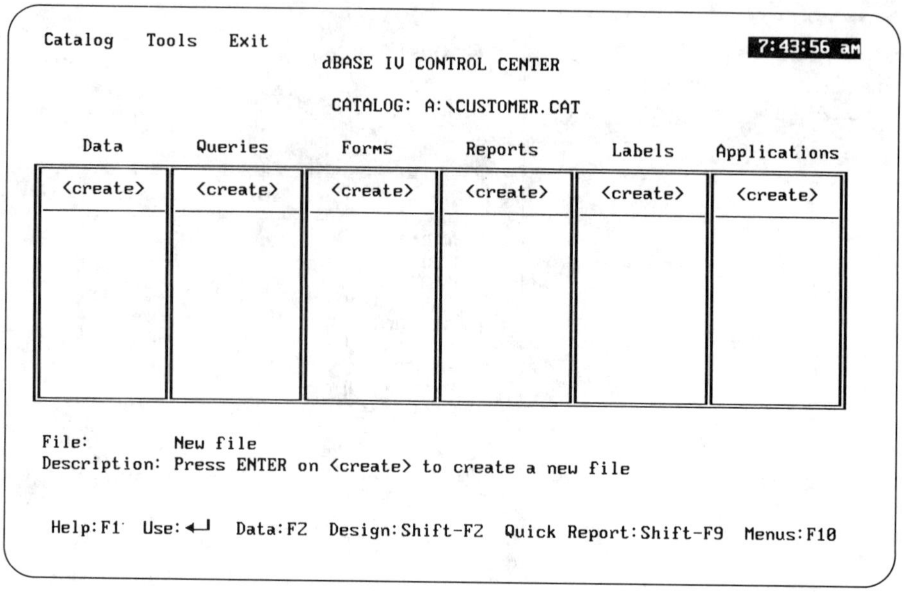

```
Catalog   Tools   Exit                                      7:43:56 am
                              dBASE IV CONTROL CENTER
                             CATALOG: A:\CUSTOMER.CAT

      Data        Queries       Forms       Reports      Labels     Applications
   ┌───────────┬───────────┬───────────┬───────────┬───────────┬───────────┐
   │ <create>  │ <create>  │ <create>  │ <create>  │ <create>  │ <create>  │
   │           │           │           │           │           │           │
   │           │           │           │           │           │           │
   │           │           │           │           │           │           │
   │           │           │           │           │           │           │
   │           │           │           │           │           │           │
   └───────────┴───────────┴───────────┴───────────┴───────────┴───────────┘

   File:        New file
   Description: Press ENTER on <create> to create a new file


    Help:F1   Use:←┘   Data:F2   Design:Shift-F2   Quick Report:Shift-F9   Menus:F10
```

Enter   Executes the command and displays a box with the prompt Enter name for new catalog:.

Type CUSTOMER   Names the catalog.

Enter   Activates the catalog (Figure 1.15). Notice that there are no files in the Data panel of the Control Center.

Add Files   The panel in which the cursor resides determines the files that are to be added. If the cursor is in the Data panel, .DBF files are added. If the cursor is in the Reports panel, report form files are added. To start, make certain that the cursor is in the Data panel.

<create>   Selects <create> in the Data panel.

F10   Invokes the menu bar.

Add file to catalog   Selects the Add file to catalog by highlighting.

Enter   Executes the command and displays a picklist menu containing the names of .DBF files (Figure 1.16).

INVENTRY.DBF   Selects INVENTRY.DBF file by highlighting.

Enter (twice)   Executes the command and leaves the description blank.

F10   Invokes the menu bar.

Add file to catalog   Selects Add file to catalog by highlighting.

Enter   Executes the command and displays a picklist menu containing the names of .DBF files (Figure 1.16).

INVTRANS   Selects the INVTRANS.DBF file by highlighting.

Enter (twice)   Executes the command and leaves the description blank.

You now have the files for the chapter examples. Your Control Center should now look like that depicted in Figure 1.17.

Figure 1.16

The picklist menu of .DBF files to be added to the CUSTOMER catalog

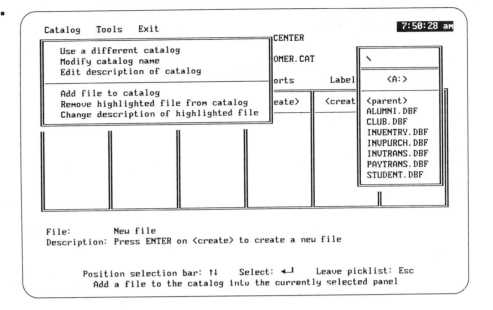

Figure 1.17

The Control Center with the added files

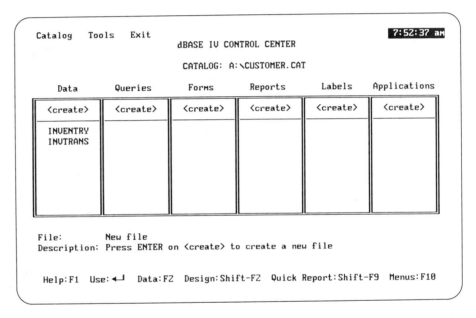

Switching Catalogs dBASE typically remembers which catalog was used last when you exit to DOS and makes that catalog the default when control is transferred to that disk device. If you want to activate a different catalog, issue the following commands:

F10 Invokes the menu bar.

Use a different catalog Selects Use a different catalog by highlighting. (It probably is already highlighted.)

Enter Executes the command.

↑ ↓ Selects the desired catalog.

Enter Executes the command.

The files in this catalog now appear in the Control Center.

HINTS/HAZARDS

Be sure that you properly exit dBASE IV via a Quit command when you have a catalog open. If you do not properly exit, the catalog file may be corrupted, and you will have to rebuild the catalog.

CREATING A dBASE IV FILE

Before dBASE IV can use a file, you must provide its name and information about its data fields (name, data type, and length) in a structure. Once the structure is created, you can enter data in the file. Use the following rules to create this structure:

1. A filename can contain up to 8 characters. Do not give the file an extension; dBASE automatically places a .DBF extension on all database files.

2. A field name can contain up to 10 characters. Acceptable characters are the letters A through Z, the digits 0 through 9, and the underscore mark (__). The **data type** to be stored in a field determines the type of field: character string (C), numeric (N), logical (L), memo (M), and date (D).

    a. A **character string field** holds any alphanumeric character (number, letter, or special character).

    b. A **numeric field** is restricted to the sign (+ or −), numerals, and the decimal point(.); the decimal point must be counted as part of the field length.

    c. A **logical field** will be marked Y (Yes) or N (No) and is always only one position in length.

    d. A **memo field** can hold a maximum of 4,096 characters and is therefore ideal for containing large amounts of text data. It appears as a field size of 10 when defined in the structure.

    e. A **date field** contains eight positions and automatically has the slashes (/) in their correct locations; an empty date field appears as __/__/__.

Let's review the CUSTOMER database application. The following 12 data items will be used to compose a data record for each customer:

First Name	Amount Owed
Middle Initial	Payment Date
Last Name	Credit Status
Address	Comments
City	
State	
ZIP	
Phone	

The Credit Status and Comments fields have been added to the record. The Credit Status will have a Y for a good credit rating and an N for a bad credit rating. The Comments field will be used to contain any information that might be pertinent for this customer (for example, likes/dislikes, favorite merchandise, birthdays of children).

Table 1.1 *Field Names, Data Types, and Field Lengths*

Field Name	Data Type	Field Lengths
FIRST	C	10
INIT	C	1
LAST	C	12
ADDRESS	C	25
CITY	C	15
STATE	C	2
ZIP	C	5
PHONE	C	13
AMOUNT	N	8,2
DATE	D	8
CR__STATUS	L	1
COMMENTS	M	10

After deciding which pieces of information to store, you must decide which type of data is to be stored in each field and how long each field should be. Character string data are used for most fields. Why would you want to use character data for the ZIP field when a ZIP code is numeric digits? A common rule of thumb is to store data as character data unless they are to be used in calculations. Also, character data are easier to include in indexing.

The Phone field is also character data because the area code appears between parentheses and a hyphen appears between the exchange and the number in that exchange. The Amount Owed, the only numeric field, has two positions to the right of the decimal point. Payment Date is a date field, Comments is a memo field, and Credit Status is a logical field. Table 1.1 shows the breakdown of field names, data types, and field lengths.

It is important not to use too many fields in a record or to define fields that are too large to hold the data. The size of the fields determines how much space they will take on disk. Unused field positions are filled with blanks. Reserving too much room for a field wastes the disk storage space.

 Creating the Structure   Creating the CUSTOMER file structure with the above fields requires using the <create> option of the Data panel. Starting at the Control Center, build the structure of the file using the following steps:

> **<create>**   Selects the ⟨ c r e a t e ⟩ option of the Data panel by highlighting.
>
> **Enter**   Displays the File creation menu (Figure 1.18).

This screen provides the necessary tools for describing to dBASE the structure of the file that you wish to build. The status line contains several pieces of information about the task being performed. The Database entry indicates that this is the panel currently invoked by dBASE. The filename is <NEW>. This name will be used by dBASE until the structure is finished and named by the user. The Field 1/1 entry indicates that you are ready to describe the first field to dBASE. The navigation line contains the instruction Enter the field name. The entry for each field provides for entering the Field Name, Field Type (data type), Width, Dec (decimal positions, if any), Index (will this field be used to create an index for the file?). Use the Dec entry only if a field

Figure 1.18

The dBASE screen used to describe a record structure to dBASE

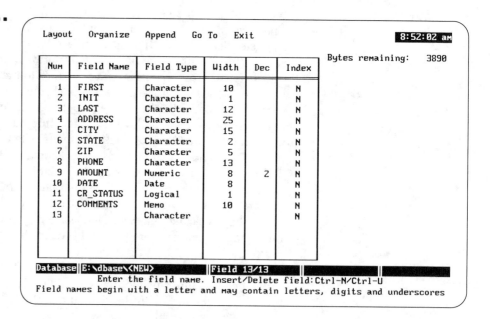

Figure 1.19

The completed dBASE structure for the CUSTOMER file

has positions to the right of the decimal. For example, if a field is designated as numeric data type 10,2; enter a 10 in the Width entry for that field and a 2 in the Dec entry.

Once the structure is created, it should appear like that depicted in Figure 1.19. To describe each field in the structure, use the following steps:

Type FIRST   Names the field.

Enter (twice)   Executes the command and accepts the Character default.

Type 10   Enters the field width.

Enter (twice)   Executes the command and indicates to dBASE that this field is not used in an index.

Continue entering the field definitions by referring to the previous list of fields.

Notes on Creating a Structure   dBASE provides several conventions for creating a structure:

1. dBASE automatically changes any alphabetic characters to upper case.
2. If you use all ten allowable characters for a field name, dBASE beeps and moves the cursor to Field Type entry.
3. You can select the Field Type by entering the first character of the data type or by pressing the Space Bar until the desired data type appears.
4. Correcting errors is a straightforward process. Use the cursor positioning keys on the keypad to move the cursor to the desired field and re-enter the data.

When you have finished entering the field descriptions, your cursor is on field 13. To terminate the structure definition, press Enter. dBASE now prompts you for the filename (Figure 1.20). Enter the name CUSTOMER and press Enter.

You should now hear some disk activity as dBASE records the file structure information to disk and creates the CUSTOMER file. It then displays the following prompt at the bottom of the screen: `Input data records now?` `(Y/N)`. Type Y.

A blank record form now appears on the screen, with the menu bar at the top of the screen (Figure 1.21). The status line shows the filename and the current record number. Each field name appears in the left-hand column next to the field itself, in reverse video to indicate its length. Fill in the appropriate blanks. When you have reached the end of a field, the computer beeps, and the cursor automatically advances to the next field. If you finish entering data before the end of the field is reached, simply press Enter. When the last field is filled or Enter is pressed, a new blank form appears. Now enter the five

. . . .

Figure 1.20

The dBASE prompt for the filename

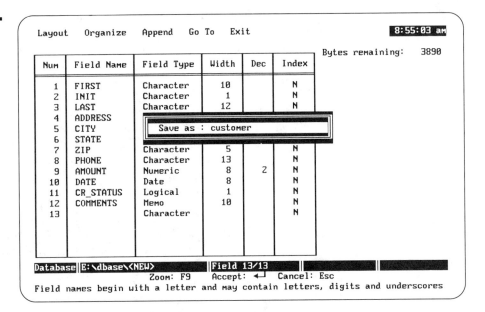

Num	Field Name	Field Type	Width	Dec	Index
1	FIRST	Character	10		N
2	INIT	Character	1		N
3	LAST	Character	12		N
4	ADDRESS				
5	CITY	Save as : customer			
6	STATE				
7	ZIP	Character	5		N
8	PHONE	Character	13		N
9	AMOUNT	Numeric	8	2	N
10	DATE	Date	8		N
11	CR_STATUS	Logical	1		N
12	COMMENTS	Memo	10		N
13		Character			N

Layout   Organize   Append   Go To   Exit   8:55:03 am

Bytes remaining: 3890

Database | E:\dbase\<NEW> | Field 13/13

Zoom: F9   Accept: ↵   Cancel: Esc

Field names begin with a letter and may contain letters, digits and underscores

● ●

Figure 1.21

Blank record form for the CUSTOMER file

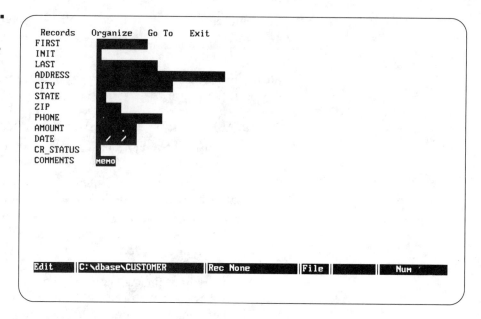

records below (don't worry about entering information in the COMMENTS field):

FIRST	INIT	LAST	ADDRESS	CITY	STATE	ZIP	PHONE	AMOUNT	DATE	CR_STATUS
Reza	R	Ghorbani	4033 N. Wolcott	Chicago	Il	60712	(312)245-0324	125.00	01/17/92	Y
Ann	B	Ghorbani	4033 N. Wolcott	Chicago	Il	60712	(312)245-0324	250.00	03/23/92	Y
Douglas	C	Acklin	408 E. Monroe	Bloomington	Il	61701	(312)663-8976	55.00	04/01/92	Y
Barbara	A	Walters	1981 Crestlawn	Arlington	Va	13411	(703)237-3727	75.00	12/31/92	Y
Arthur	V	Adams	115 Ginger Creek Ct.	Bloomington	Il	61701	(309)828-7290	35.00	03/13/92	Y

When you enter numeric information, dBASE automatically right-justifies the number in the field when you press Enter. If the number does not have decimal positions, do not enter a decimal point; dBASE automatically places it in the appropriate location.

When this form has been filled with the data for the first record, it should look like the screen in Figure 1.22.

As each record is entered, dBASE places a new, empty form on the screen and raises the record number in the status bar. When you have finished entering all five records, press Enter at the next blank form. dBASE then assumes that you have finished entering data and returns you to the Control Center. If you press Enter prematurely and are returned to the Control Center, issue the following commands:

Shift + F2   Issues the Design command.

Append   Selects the Append command by highlighting.

Enter   Executes the command.

When you have finished adding records, issue the following commands:

Figure 1.22

Filled-in form for the first data record of the CUSTOMER.DBF file

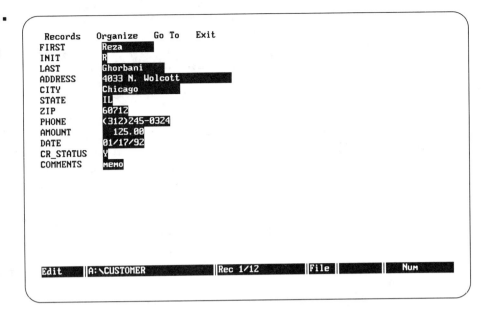

```
    Records    Organize    Go To    Exit
    FIRST      Reza
    INIT       R
    LAST       Ghorbani
    ADDRESS    4033 N. Wolcott
    CITY       Chicago
    STATE      IL
    ZIP        60712
    PHONE      (312)245-0324
    AMOUNT        125.00
    DATE       01/17/92
    CR_STATUS  Y
    COMMENTS   memo




   Edit    ║A:\CUSTOMER              ║Rec 1/12    ║File ║        ║  Num
```

Figure 1.23

The file displayed using the dBASE tabular format

```
    Records    Organize    Fields    Go To    Exit
   ┌─────────┬────┬────────┬────────────────────┬────────────┬─────┬─┐
   │FIRST    │INIT│LAST    │ADDRESS             │CITY        │STATE│Z│
   ├─────────┼────┼────────┼────────────────────┼────────────┼─────┼─┤
   │Reza     │R   │Ghorbani│4033 N. Wolcott     │Chicago     │Il   │6│
   │Ann      │B   │Ghorbani│4033 N. Wolcott     │Chicago     │Il   │6│
   │Douglas  │C   │Acklin  │408 E. Monroe       │Bloomington │Il   │6│
   │Barbara  │A   │Walters │1981 Crestlawn      │Arlington   │Va   │1│
   │Arthur   │V   │Adams   │115 Ginger Creek Ct.│Bloomington │Il   │6│
   │         │    │        │                    │            │     │ │
   └─────────┴────┴────────┴────────────────────┴────────────┴─────┴─┘
   Browse   ║C:\dbase\CUSTOMER         ║Rec 1/5    ║File ║        ║ NumCaps
```

F10   Selects the Menu bar.

Exit   Selects the E x i t command by highlighting.

Save changes and exit   Selects S a v e   c h a n g e s   a n d   e x i t.

Enter (twice)   Executes the command and returns you to the Control Center.

Once you have issued the Append command via the Shift + F2 key sequence, you can access an empty form by highlighting the CUSTOMER file and pressing F2 or pressing Enter and selecting the D i s p l a y d a t a option. Prior to that time, you receive the contents of the file in the form of a table (Figure 1.23). You can also use this row/column form for adding records to your file.

If you note errors in a record, you can correct them using standard editing conventions. A record is recorded to the file any time that a Pg Up or Pg Dn key is pressed when you are filling in a form. You can also use these keys to view the records in the file to ensure that there are no errors.

ACTIVATING THE DATABASE

You have now created the CUSTOMER database file and recorded five records in it. If you are still in dBASE and have not activated any other files, to add records to the CUSTOMER file just enter the commands for appending records.

If you quit dBASE and later want to add records to the CUSTOMER file, you must re-enter dBASE and perform some or all of the following steps:

1. Reset the default drive.
2. Activate the file.
3. Issue the series of commands for appending records.

Once a file has been activated and the Control Center is on the screen, you can look at the structure of the file by pressing Shift + F2 and then Esc. This series of commands displays the structure of the file (Figure 1.24). Once you have obtained the needed information, press Esc again and respond Yes to the abandon prompt to return to the Control Center.

You can also obtain a structure of the file by issuing the List Structure command from the dot prompt (Figure 1.25). This listing numbers the fields and provides a total number of bytes used by the structure.

As Figure 1.25 shows, dBASE keeps track of the current number of records in the file and includes the .DBF extension in the filename. If the date was entered properly when you booted DOS, dBASE also keeps track of the date of the last update; if it wasn't, the date will be 01/01/80. You can also see the name, character type, and width of each field. The total bytes of storage used by each record are at the bottom of the listing. The total number of bytes is one more than the sum of the individual field sizes, to reserve a position for the delete indicator (*).

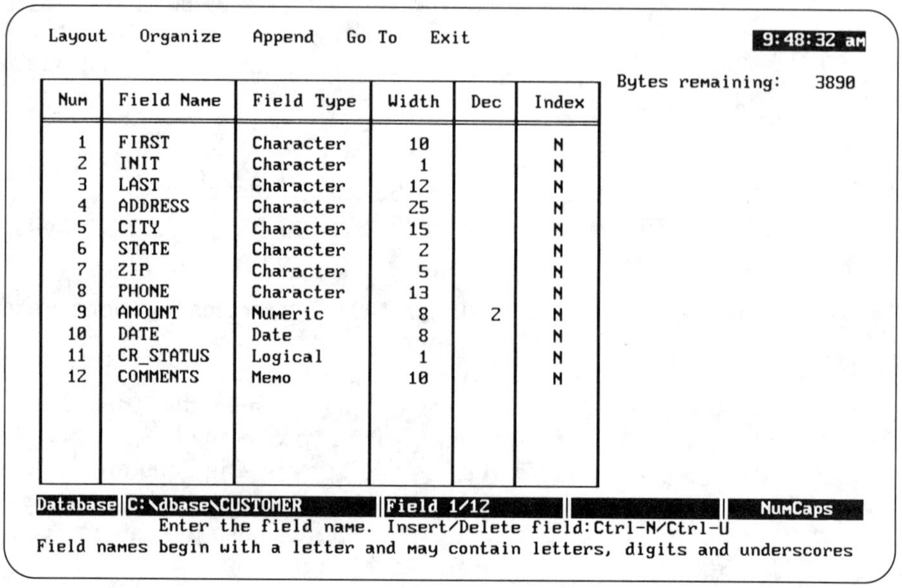

Figure 1.24

The file structure can be obtained from the Shift + F2 (Design) command

Layout	Organize	Append	Go To	Exit			9:48:32 am

Bytes remaining: 3890

Num	Field Name	Field Type	Width	Dec	Index
1	FIRST	Character	10		N
2	INIT	Character	1		N
3	LAST	Character	12		N
4	ADDRESS	Character	25		N
5	CITY	Character	15		N
6	STATE	Character	2		N
7	ZIP	Character	5		N
8	PHONE	Character	13		N
9	AMOUNT	Numeric	8	2	N
10	DATE	Date	8		N
11	CR_STATUS	Logical	1		N
12	COMMENTS	Memo	10		N

Database	C:\dbase\CUSTOMER	Field 1/12		NumCaps

Enter the field name. Insert/Delete field:Ctrl-N/Ctrl-U
Field names begin with a letter and may contain letters, digits and underscores

Figure 1.25

The structure obtained from the dot prompt using the List Structure command

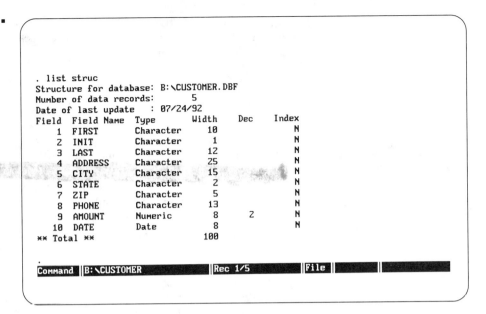

```
. list struc
Structure for database: B:\CUSTOMER.DBF
Number of data records:        5
Date of last update   : 07/24/92
Field  Field Name  Type       Width   Dec   Index
    1   FIRST       Character     10            N
    2   INIT        Character      1            N
    3   LAST        Character     12            N
    4   ADDRESS     Character     25            N
    5   CITY        Character     15            N
    6   STATE       Character      2            N
    7   ZIP         Character      5            N
    8   PHONE       Character     13            N
    9   AMOUNT      Numeric        8      2     N
   10   DATE        Date           8            N
** Total **                      100
```

```
Command  B:\CUSTOMER        Rec 1/5        File
```

Figure 1.26

The screen display of a report using the CUSTOMER file

```
Page No.   1
07/24/92

FIRST     INIT  LAST      ADDRESS            CITY           STAT
E  ZIP    PHONE           AMOUNT  DATE


Reza       R    Ghorbani     4033 N. Wolcott   Chicago        Il
   60712  (312)245-0324   125.00  01/17/91
Ann        B    Ghorbani     4033 N. Wolcott   Chicago        Il
   60712  (312)245-0324   250.00  03/23/91
Douglas    C    Acklin        408 E. Monroe    Bloomington    Il
   61701  (312)663-8976    55.00  04/01/91
Barbara    A    Walters      1981 Crestlawn    Arlington      Va
   13411  (703)237-3727    75.00  12/31/91
Arthur     V    Adams         115 Ginger Creek Ct. Bloomington Il
   61701  (309)828-7290    35.00  03/13/91

                           540.00



        Cancel viewing: ESC,  Continue viewing: SPACEBAR
```

Listing Records   Once a file is created, you can use the dBASE **Quick Report command** (Shift + F9) to generate a report of the records that can be displayed to your monitor or dumped to a printer for later review. Displaying a report to the screen is accomplished using the following commands:

Shift + F9   Issues the Quick Report command.

View report on screen   Selects View report on screen by highlighting.

Enter   Displays the report depicted in Figure 1.26 on the screen, after a few seconds. Press the Space Bar several times to see the rest of the listing.

The report starts at the beginning of the data file and lists all records to the screen. For readability, dBASE lists the field names above the data and continues displaying records until the screen is filled. It displays the field names as the first line(s) of the report. If a line is too long, it is wrapped to the next line. dBASE automatically keeps track of the page number, date, and generating totals for numeric fields.

ADDING RECORDS TO THE FILE

To add records to the database file, issue the **Design command** (Shift + F2) and then select the **Append command** from the menu bar. Any records added to a file via the Append command are placed at the end of the existing file. When the Append command executes, dBASE performs a number of actions: The screen clears and displays a blank record form, the record number in the status bar is updated for the new record, and the monitor displays a blank entry screen (Figure 1.27).

You can now enter records to the end of the file, as you did after the file was initially created. As soon as you fill the last field of this form or press Enter when the cursor is in the last field, dBASE automatically displays the next blank record form.

When you have finished adding new records, indicate this by pressing Enter at the start of the next blank form.

Add the following records to the CUSTOMER.DBF file:

FIRST	INIT	LAST	ADDRESS	CITY	STATE	ZIP	PHONE	AMOUNT	DATE	CR_STATUS
Russell	B	Davis	707 Vale St.	Bloomington	Il	61701	(309)662-1759	35.00	02/27/91	Y
Debbie	C	Acklin	408 E. Monroe	Bloomington	Il	61701	(309)827-1395	35.00	03/21/92	Y
Harvey	B	Posio	1013 Hillcrest	San Diego	Ca	94307	(619)271-9871	1250.00	04/03/92	Y
Ben	A	Pietrowiak	3334 N. Foster	Normal	Il	61761	(309)452-9126	20.00	03/23/92	Y
Sandy	C	Akclin	408 E. Monroe	Bloomington	Il	61701	(309)829-9901	35.00	02/25/91	Y
Fred	R	Ficek	1215 Tamarack	Normal	Il	61761	(309)454-7123	0.00	04/05/91	Y
Juan	C	Decesario	1214 Flores	Miami	Fl	12562	(305)719-1363	10.00	04/01/91	Y

After entering these records, check for errors by using the Quick Report command and printing the records. Your report should appear like that depicted in Figure 1.28.

EDITING RECORDS IN THE FILE

There should be 12 records in the file. Examine each record for errors. Notice that in record 10 the last name is spelled incorrectly. To correct this, use the following commands:

CUSTOMER   Selects the CUSTOMER file in the Data panel.

Enter   Executes the command.

Display data   Selects the Display data option of the menu box.

Enter   Executes the command.

Pg Up or Pg Dn   Positions the cursor to the desired record (Figure 1.29).

The contents of the last record in the file should now be displayed.

Figure 1.27

The Append screen

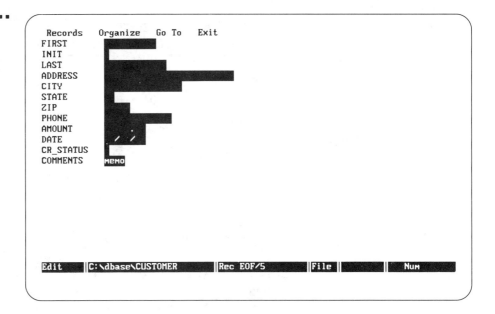

Figure 1.28

The printed report of the CUSTOMER file

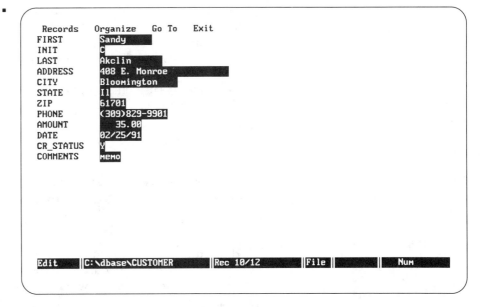

Figure 1.29

A screen for record 10 of the CUS-TOMER file

Table 1.2 Cursor Movement Within a Record

Cursor Control Key	dBASE Command	Cursor Movement or Function
⏎	Enter	Moves to next field or record.
	Ctrl + A	Moves one word to the left.
	Ctrl + F	Moves one word to the right.
←	Ctrl + S	Moves one position to the left.
→	Ctrl + D	Moves one position to the right.
↑	Ctrl + E	Moves up one line; at top line, displays prior record.
↓	Ctrl + X	Moves one line; at bottom line, displays next record.
Del	Ctrl + G	Deletes character at cursor position and moves text one position to the left.

Cursor Movement Within a Record   Various commands let you move around within a record to edit selected fields. To move the cursor from one field to the next, press Enter. Table 1.2 shows other commands you can use. To correct the error in record 10, do the following:

Enter   (or Down Arrow twice)   Moves the cursor to the LAST field, by pressing either key twice.

Right Arrow   Positions the cursor at the *k*.

Type *ck*   Makes the correction.

Ctrl + End   Saves the correction and returns to the control center.

If you are a WordStar user, you may have noticed that the movement commands in the middle column of Table 1.2 are the same as those for WordStar.

Entering Data in a Memo Field   The CUSTOMER database has a structure that includes a COMMENTS field with a data type of memo. None of the records has yet used this field. A memo field is a field that belongs to a different (memo) file and can store and link text-oriented data with a database record. This is necessary because every record in a database file will not necessarily require this text-oriented data, which uses vast amounts of record space.

Suppose that you want to add information to Reza Ghorbani's record using the COMMENTS field. Bring the record to the screen using the appropriate positioning command and then position to the COMMENTS field. Issue the following commands and then enter the comment:

Down Arrow   Positions to the COMMENTS field. Notice that the entry in this field is memo.

Ctrl + Home   Opens the memo field (Figure 1.30). Enter the following comment:

```
Reza has several hobbies. One that is of spe-
cial interest is sky diving. Over the last few
years he has made enough jumps to reach instruc-
tor status. He also enjoys driving sports cars.
He has two daughters.
```

Ctrl + End   Saves the comments. Notice that the entry in the COMMENTS field is now MEMO. The upper case indicates that the memo field of this record now has something in it.

Ctrl + End   Saves the file and returns to the Control Center.

Figure 1.30

A sample memo screen

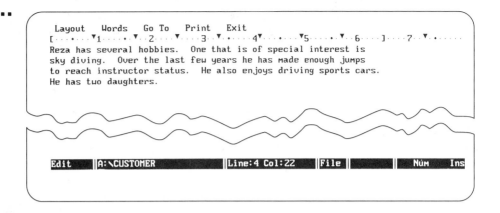

```
 Layout   Words   Go To   Print   Exit
[....▼1....▼..2....▼..3.▼...4▼....▼5....▼..6....]....?.▼......
Reza has several hobbies.  One that is of special interest is
sky diving.  Over the last few years he has made enough jumps
to reach instructor status.  He also enjoys driving sports cars.
He has two daughters.
```

```
Edit    A:\CUSTOMER                 Line:4 Col:22    File            Num   Ins
```

dBASE IV FILE TYPES

As noted earlier, dBASE automatically places a .DBF file extension on any file created by dBASE. dBASE also generates other files. The following gives the name and file extension of several commonly found files, along with a brief description. Many are discussed later in more detail.

Database Files (.DBF)   Database files consist of records that contain information about a business happening or transaction and comprise fields of data.

Memo Files (.DBT)   Memo files store the large blocks of information found in the memo fields of a database file. The information in a memo field is actually stored in a separate file.

Index Files (.NDX)   Index files let dBASE appear to arrange information in a file without actually sorting it.

Format Files (.FMT)   Format files store custom screen forms or custom report forms.

Label Files (.LBL)   Label files are used for printing labels with the Label command.

Memory Files (.MEM)   Memory files store the active memory variables to disk. A memory variable represents a temporary memory location that can hold the result of one or more computations.

Report Form Files (.FRM)   Report form files hold the parameters used to create a stored report form.

Text Files (.TXT)   Text files hold data that have been copied from a database file to this temporary file. This lets other application packages (such as word processing packages) access these data.

Catalog Files (.CAT)   Catalog files contain all names of a set of related database files and their related files.

Query Files (.QRY)   Query files contain information about the conditions for displaying records from an existing database file.

Screen Files (.SCR)   Screen files contain information about the screen layout of a custom data-entry form.

View Files (.VUE)   View files are used for relating database files with their related indexes, format fields, and other information defining the relationships among all these files.

. . . .

CHAPTER REVIEW

The term *database* is usually synonymous with *file* when microcomputers are involved in processing data. A database consists of records that hold information about some type of business entity or transaction. Each record contains pieces of data, called fields, that relate to the transaction.

When designing the format of the file to hold data, you must design it to handle future processing needs. This may mean separating name fields into last name, first name, and middle initial fields so that the computer can arrange the information in alphabetic order by last name.

The dBASE IV package is a combination menu-driven and command-driven software package. It places a number of limitations on files, including limitations on total records in a file, record size, number of fields in a record, and it must be run from hard disk.

Before creating a dBASE file, you must plan the field name, the field length, and the type of data to be used for each field and place this in the structure of the file. The structure is built by accessing the <create> option of the Data panel on the Control Center. Once the structure is built, you have the option of adding records to the file immediately or waiting until later.

You may want to change the default drive/directory so that files will be saved to a disk other than that containing the dBASE files. Do this by using the Tools option of the menu bar.

Listing records to the screen requires issuing the Quick Report command and directing the output to the screen rather than to the printer.

Changing a record requires using one of three different methods. The screen displays the last record accessed. Various dBASE commands using the Ctrl key as well as cursor keys on the numeric keypad can position the cursor and move from one record to the next within the file.

. . . .

KEY TERMS AND CONCEPTS

Append command
Catalog
character string field
Command
COMMAND mode
command-driven mode
Condition
CONTROL CENTER mode
data type
database
date field
Design command
dBASE II
dBASE III
dBASE III Plus
dBASE IV
dot prompt
field
file information

Help command
logical field
memo field
menu bar
menu-driven mode
message line
navigation line
Noun
numeric field
Panels
primary key
PROGRAM mode
Quick Report command
Quit command
record
Scope
secondary key
status bar
structure

CHAPTER QUIZ

Multiple Choice

1. Which of the following is *not* a true statement about dBASE IV?
   a. The package can be used only in MENU mode.
   b. No statements can be saved to a file and executed later.
   c. Once the dot prompt is reached, the Control Center cannot be reactivated.
   d. All of the above statements are false.

2. Which of the following commands lets you place records in a database file?
   a. Use
   b. <create>
   c. List
   d. Append
   e. Add

3. The Quick Print command is used for the following:
   a. Looking at records contained in a file
   b. Invoking a database file
   c. Displaying the structure of a database file
   d. Exiting the dBASE IV program
   e. Making changes to a file

4. Which of the following commands lets you make a change to an existing database file?
   a. Append
   b. List
   c. Use
   d. Create
   e. Quit

5. Which of the following are valid data types for use with dBASE IV?
   a. Character
   b. Numeric
   c. Memo
   d. Date
   e. Logical
   f. All of the above

True/False

6. The dBASE IV package, using the Control Center, is menu-driven. T

7. The dBASE IV package uses the period (.) as the default user prompt. F

8. It is advisable to use the Quit command from the dot prompt or the Quit to DOS from the Exit option of the menu bar to avoid data loss. T

9. The dBASE IV package makes use of the cursor pad as well as WordStar-like commands for cursor manipulation. T

10. The Append command lets you access and change any field of a record. T

Answers

1. d   2. b, d   3. a   4. a   5. f   6. t   7. f   8. t   9. t   10. t

Exercises

1. Define or describe each of the following:
   a. command-driven   c. structure
   b. menu-driven

2. The maximum number of records allowed in a dBASE IV file is $\underline{1\ billion}$.

3. The line of the Control Center menu that indicates the current disk drive and the name of the file in use is the $\underline{File\ Information}$ line.

4. Invoke the Help command by pressing the _____$F1$_____ function key.

5. Before you turn off the computer, you must issue the _____$Quit$_____ command to avoid data loss.

6. Press the _____ESC_____ key to exit the Control Center menu to the dot prompt.

7. The default mode for dBASE is the $\underline{Control\ Center}$ menu.

8. A dBASE record can have up to _____4000_____ characters.

9. Use the $\underline{Create}$ _____ command of the Data panel to describe a record to dBASE.

10. A file is made available to dBASE highlighting the filename in the $\underline{Catalogue}$ of the Control Center.

11. The $\underline{Primary\ Key}$ gives the physical location (record number) of a record in a file.

12. The $\underline{F10 + Exit}$ should be used to exit dBASE.

13. Use the $\underline{.list struc}$ command at the dot prompt to look at the structure of a dBASE file.

14. Use the _____$Append$_____ command to add data to an existing database file.

15. Activate the Control Center at the command level by using the $\underline{assist}$ command.

COMPUTER EXERCISES

1. Create a catalog called PROJECTS, which you will use for all end-of-chapter projects. Remember that to place project files in this catalog automatically, dBASE has to be told to use this catalog via the Catalog submenu. Once the catalog is created, add the following files to the catalog:

   ```
   ALUMNI
   CLUB
   PAYTRANS
   STUDENT
   ```

2. Create a file called PAYMAST. It should have the following structure:

NAME	TYPE	WIDTH	DEC
EMPLOY_ID	N	004	
FIRSTNAM	C	010	
LASTNAM	C	012	
PAYRATE	N	006	002
YTDGROSS	N	009	002

3. Enter the following records:

ID	NAME	RATE	GROSS
4908	Richard Payne	4.45	556.00
5789	Connie Reiners	3.35	450.00
5323	Pamela Rich	6.00	780.00
6324	Mark Tell	5.50	980.00
2870	Frank Terlep	3.80	670.00
4679	Kenneth Klass	4.90	780.00
8345	Thomas Momery	4.70	580.00

4. List the contents of the file by using the Quick Report command. - Print

5. Add the records below:

5649	Toni McCarthy	5.20	667.00
5432	Alan Monroe	5.20	1340.00
5998	Paul Mish	4.90	887.00
4463	Edward Mockford	4.90	775.00
456		0.00	0.00

6. Use the Display data, Append, or ~~Date~~ Edit command to correct any errors. Also use the ~~Edit~~ command to place your name in the name area for record 12.

7. Invoke the CLUB file. Select Display data and use the Browse screen to examine the file.

BROWSE, FILE MANIPULATION, SORTING, INDEXING, AND LOCATING RECORDS

CHAPTER OBJECTIVES

After completing this chapter, you should be able to:

- Use the Browse command
- Enter commands using both the Control Center and the dot prompt
- Use a number of data manipulation commands
- Locate records in an unordered database
- Use the Sort command
- Use the Index command
- Delete unwanted index files
- Locate records in an ordered (indexed) file

This chapter introduces the Browse command and a number of file manipulation commands and shows how to sort files, create indexes, and locate records in both unordered and ordered files. These commands are covered using the Control Center as well as the command level (dot prompt).

USING THE DOT PROMPT

Many individuals who have used dBASE for a period of time decide that they want to enter commands at the dot prompt rather than use the Control Center menus. Most of the dBASE examples feature the use of the Control Center. The dot prompt commands for the exercises are given for each of the menu examples. If a dot prompt command that provides you with flexibility and power is not found in a Control Center menu, it will be covered in detail.

CORRECTING ERRORS AT THE DOT PROMPT

From time to time, you will enter a command that violates the dBASE syntax and generates an error menu box on the screen. Such a box generally contains three options: Cancel, Edit, and Help. Cancel returns you to the dot prompt. Edit lets you change the statement while keeping the error box on the screen. Help displays information about the command.

If the statement is fairly long and complex, you can also select Cancel and then obtain the instruction from the history buffer by pressing the Up Arrow key. The history buffer, unless the default has been changed, can hold up to 20 instructions. Once the command appears at the dot prompt, it can be changed using editing commands and executed by pressing Enter.

Remember, you activate COMMAND mode (the dot prompt) by pressing Esc one or more times from the Control Center and responding Yes to the prompt `Are you sure you want to abandon operation?`

BROWSE

The **Browse command** and its display screen is dBASE's main method of displaying records of an invoked (used) file. Use the Browse screen, like the Edit command, to make any desired changes to a file. Many dBASE commands display their results using the Browse screen. It is therefore important that you understand how various commands work with this screen. The usual method of invoking this screen is by highlighting a file, pressing Enter, highlighting the menu option `Display data`, and pressing Enter. You can also invoke this screen from the Control Center by highlighting a file and pressing F2.

Use the commands in Chapter 1 to change the default drive to A or whichever drive you are using (`.SET DEFAULT TO A:`). Invoke the CUSTOMER file using the following commands:

CUSTOMER   Selects the `CUSTOMER` file.

Enter   Executes the command.

Display data   Selects the `Display data` option.

Enter   Executes the command.

Figure 2.1

The CUSTOMER file displayed on the Browse screen

```
Records   Organize   Fields   Go To   Exit

FIRST      INIT LAST      ADDRESS                CITY          STATE Z

Reza       R    Ghorbani  4033 N. Wolcott        Chicago       Il   6
Ann        B    Ghorbani  4033 N. Wolcott        Chicago       Il   6
Douglas    C    Acklin    408 E. Monroe          Bloomington   Il   6
Barbara    A    Walters   1981 Crestlaun         Arlington     Va   1
Arthur     U    Adams     115 Ginger Creek Ct.   Bloomington   Il   6
Russell    B    Davis     707 Vale St.           Bloomington   Il   6
Debbie     C    Acklin    408 E. Monroe          Bloomington   Il   6
Harvey     B    Posio     1013 Hillcrest         San Diego     Ca   9
Ben        A    Pietrowiak 3334 N. Foster        Normal        Il   6
Sandy      C    Acklin    408 E. Monroe          Bloomington   Il   6
Fred       R    Ficek     1215 Tamarack          Normal        Il   6
Juan       C    Decesario 1214 Flores            Miami         Fl   1

Browse   A:\CUSTOMER          Rec 1/12      File          Num
```

CURSOR MOVEMENT

Once the Browse screen appears (Figure 2.1), you can use three function key commands:

F2 Shifts between that display and Edit.

Esc Exits Browse.

F10 Displays the menu bar.

When the Browse screen is present, you can use many of the cursor movement commands discussed in Chapter 1 to move through the file. Only those commands that have differences are discussed below:

- *Enter* moves left to right one field at a time (each field appears as a line within a column). As you can see, all fields contained in the CUSTOMER file will not fit on your screen. As you continue to press Enter, fields that were not previously visible appear. This is known as **panning.** As panning occurs, fields that were previously visible are replaced with the new fields.

- *Arrow Keys* allow movement within a field and a file. The Left and Right Arrow keys move the cursor one character at a time within a field. When the end of the field is reached, the cursor jumps to the next field. The Up and Down Arrows move, respectively, up or down one record at a time within the file.

- *Home* moves the cursor to the beginning of a record.

- *Tab* functions much like Enter. It moves to the right a field at a time. The Shift + Tab moves to the left a field at a time.

- *Pg Up* and *Pg Dn* move the cursor up or down a screen through the file. There is always an overlap of one record from one screen to the next.

• •

Figure 2.2

The Browse screen with the resized
ADDRESS field

| Records | Organize | Fields | Go To | Exit |

FIRST	INIT	LAST	ADDRESS	CITY	STATE	ZIP	P
Reza	R	Ghorbani	4033 N. Wolcott	Chicago	Il	60712	‹
Ann	B	Ghorbani	4033 N. Wolcott	Chicago	Il	60712	‹
Douglas	C	Acklin	408 E. Monroe	Bloomington	Il	61701	‹
Barbara	A	Walters	1981 Crestlawn	Arlington	Va	13411	‹
Arthur	V	Adams	115 Ginger Creek Ct	Bloomington	Il	61701	‹
Russell	B	Davis	707 Vale St.	Bloomington	Il	61701	‹
Debbie	C	Acklin	408 E. Monroe	Bloomington	Il	61701	‹
Harvey	B	Posio	1013 Hillcrest	San Diego	Ca	94307	‹
Ben	A	Pietrowiak	3334 N. Foster	Normal	Il	61761	‹
Sandy	C	Acklin	408 E. Monroe	Bloomington	Il	61701	‹
Fred	R	Ficek	1215 Tamarack	Normal	Il	61761	‹
Juan	C	Decesario	1214 Flores	Miami	Fl	12562	‹

| Browse | A:\CUSTOMER | | Rec 1/12 | | File | | Num |

- *Ctrl + End* saves all changes and returns you to the Control Center.
- *Esc* aborts editing of the current record only and thereby omits changes for the current record and returns you to the Control Center.

CHANGING COLUMN DISPLAY WIDTH

When you are using Browse, you may want to resize one or more columns on the screen so that additional fields can appear on the screen. Do this by using the **Size field option** of the Fields menu. When resizing a column/field on the screen, only the display is altered. The file remains unchanged. The field that is resized is the field at the cursor location. Suppose you want to resize the ADDRESS field. After positioning the cursor to that field, enter the following instructions:

F10 Invokes the menu bar.

Fields Selects the F i e l d s option.

Size field Selects S i z e f i e l d.

Enter Executes the command.

← (6 times) Resizes the field.

Enter Executes the command. The field is now resized (Figure 2.2). As a result the ZIP field is now visible.

FREEZING A FIELD

Suppose that you want to make a change to the same field of each record. When you are using Browse and change a field, dBASE may take you to the next field of the record or perform some other type of undesirable cursor movement. The **Freeze field option** of the Fields menu solves this problem.

Figure 2.3

The corrected STATE field contents

```
 Records   Organize   Fields   Go To   Exit

 FIRST      INIT LAST       ADDRESS             CITY         STATE ZIP    P

 Reza       R    Ghorbani   4033 N. Wolcott     Chicago      IL    60712 <
 Ann        B    Ghorbani   4033 N. Wolcott     Chicago      IL    60712 <
 Douglas    C    Acklin     408 E. Monroe       Bloomington  IL    61701 <
 Barbara    A    Walters    1981 Crestlawn      Arlington    VA    13411 <
 Arthur     U    Adams      115 Ginger Creek Ct Bloomington  IL    61701 <
 Russell    B    Davis      707 Vale St.        Bloomington  IL    61701 <
 Debbie     C    Acklin     408 E. Monroe       Bloomington  IL    61701 <
 Harvey     B    Posio      1013 Hillcrest      San Diego    CA    94307 <
 Ben        A    Pietrowiak 3334 N. Foster      Normal       IL    61761 <
 Sandy      C    Acklin     408 E. Monroe       Bloomington  IL    61701 <
 Fred       R    Ficek      1215 Tamarack       Normal       IL    61761 <
 Juan       C    Decesario  1214 Flores         Miami        FL    12562 <




 Browse  ║A:\CUSTOMER            ║║Rec 12/12     ║║File ║║     ║║  NumCaps ║
```

 Suppose that you had forgotten to capitalize the second character of the STATE field for each record. This is corrected using the following commands:

> **F10**   Invokes the menu bar.
>
> **Fields**   Selects the F i e l d s option.
>
> **Freeze field**   Selects F r e e z e   f i e l d.
>
> **Enter**   Executes the command.
>
> **Type STATE**   Names the field to freeze.
>
> **Enter**   Executes the command.

Now, when changes are made to the record, the cursor moves to the same field of the next record. At this time, change each of the lowercase characters in the STATE field to uppercase characters (Figure 2.3).

To turn off the Freeze option, do the following:

> **F10**   Invokes the menu bar.
>
> **Fields**   Selects the F i e l d s option.
>
> **Freeze field**   Selects F r e e z e   f i e l d.
>
> **Enter**   Executes the command.
>
> **Backspace (5 times)**   Erases the field name.
>
> **Enter**   Executes the command.

If you want to use the Browse field command from the dot prompt, enter the command BROWSE. When you enter this command, you receive all fields and have to pan to see fields that are not visible. You can limit the number of fields included in a browse session by including the Fields entry and listing the fields to be included. For instance, the following Browse command at the dot prompt limits the fields to those depicted in Figure 2.4.

.BROWSE FIELDS FIRST,LAST,ADDRESS,STATE,AMOUNT

. . . .

Figure 2.4

The output of the Browse fields command

```
 Records   Organize   Fields   Go To   Exit

 ┌─────────┬──────────┬──────────────────────┬───────┬────────┐
 │ FIRST   │ LAST     │ ADDRESS              │ STATE │ AMOUNT │
 ├─────────┼──────────┼──────────────────────┼───────┼────────┤
 │ Reza    │ Ghorbani │ 4033 N. Wolcott      │ IL    │  125.00│
 │ Ann     │ Ghorbani │ 4033 N. Wolcott      │ IL    │  250.00│
 │ Douglas │ Acklin   │ 408 E. Monroe        │ IL    │   55.00│
 │ Barbara │ Walters  │ 1981 Crestlawn       │ VA    │   75.00│
 │ Arthur  │ Adams    │ 115 Ginger Creek Ct. │ IL    │   35.00│
 │ Russell │ Davis    │ 707 Vale St.         │ IL    │   35.00│
 │ Debbie  │ Acklin   │ 408 E. Monroe        │ IL    │   35.00│
 │ Harvey  │ Posio    │ 1013 Hillcrest       │ CA    │ 1250.00│
 │ Ben     │ Pietrowiak│ 3334 N. Foster      │ IL    │   20.00│
 │ Sandy   │ Acklin   │ 408 E. Monroe        │ IL    │   35.00│
 │ Fred    │ Ficek    │ 1215 Tamarack        │ IL    │    0.00│
 │ Juan    │ Decesario│ 1214 Flores          │ FL    │   10.00│
 │         │          │                      │       │        │
 └─────────┴──────────┴──────────────────────┴───────┴────────┘
 Browse    A:\CUSTOMER              Rec 1/12      File         NumCaps
```

ADDING NEW RECORDS

When the cursor is positioned beyond the last record in the Browse table, dBASE displays the prompt Add new records? (Y/N) at the bottom of the screen. If you respond Y, the message Add new records appears, and any records that are entered from the keyboard are appended to the file. If the contents of a field from the prior record are desired in the same field of the record being added, press Shift + F8 to copy the data to the current field.

. . . .

FILE MANIPULATION COMMANDS AND SEARCHING UNORDERED FILES

This section introduces a number of dBASE file manipulation commands that can be accessed from the menu bar once a file has been invoked. In addition, we discuss locating records from unordered files.

RECORD POINTER

Recall from Chapter 1 that dBASE uses a **record pointer** to keep track of where it is within a file. The record number that appears in the status bar of the screen when you are appending or editing records is the current location of the pointer. Many commands that are given to dBASE result in this pointer moving from one location (record) in a file to another location.

The following examples using the CUSTOMER file illustrate dBASE's tracking of the pointer. Use the commands in Chapter 1 to change the default drive to A or whichever drive you are using (.SET DEFAULT TO A:). Invoke the CUSTOMER file using the following commands:

CUSTOMER Selects the CUSTOMER file in the Data panel (.USE CUSTOMER).

Enter Executes the command.

Figure 2.5

The Rec entry of the status bar contains the pointer position within a file

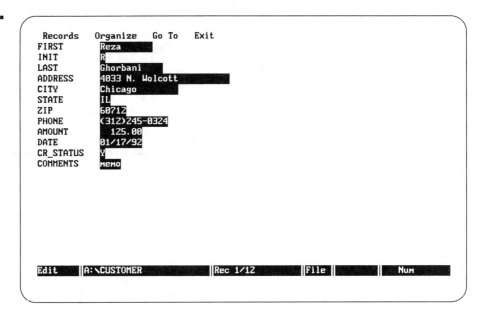

```
    Records    Organize    Go To    Exit
    FIRST      Reza
    INIT       R
    LAST       Ghorbani
    ADDRESS    4033 N. Wolcott
    CITY       Chicago
    STATE      IL
    ZIP        60712
    PHONE      (312)245-0324
    AMOUNT         125.00
    DATE       01/17/92
    CR_STATUS  Y
    COMMENTS   memo
```

| Edit | A:\CUSTOMER | Rec 1/12 | File | | Num |

Display data Selects the D i s p l a y d a t a option (.EDIT).

Enter Executes the command and displays the CUSTOMER file in tabular format.

F2 Goes to EDIT mode.

You should now see a screen similar to the one depicted in Figure 2.5. Notice that the status bar contains the entry R e c 1 / 1 2. This is the current position of the pointer. You can position the pointer to other records by using Pg Up and Pg Dn keys. Press Pg Dn three times. Notice that the Rec entry of the status bar now has the value 4/12, indicating that the pointer is now positioned to record 4.

Using Pg Up and Pg Dn to position the pointer is adequate when using files that contain few records. If you had several thousand records in a file, however, such pointer positioning commands would take far too long. A faster way to move the pointer within a file is to use the Go To option in the menu bar (Figure 2.6). The Top record option positions the pointer to the beginning of the file. The Last record option positions the pointer at the end of the file. The Record number option gives the current pointer location and lets you go to a specific record.

To invoke this option, issue the following commands:

F10 Invokes the menu bar.

Go To Selects the G o T o option.

Last record Selects the L a s t r e c o r d option.

Enter Executes the command. The pointer should now be at record 12—check the Rec entry of the status bar (.GOTO BOTTOM).

F10 Invokes the menu bar and the Go To menu. Notice that the Record number entry contains the value { 1 2 } (the current pointer location).

Top record Selects the F i r s t r e c o r d option (.GOTO TOP).

Enter Executes the command. The pointer should now be at record 1.

· ·

Figure 2.6

The Go To menu

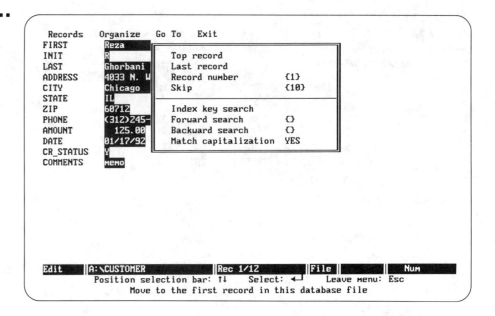

Figure 2.7

The Go To screen for positioning directly to a specified record

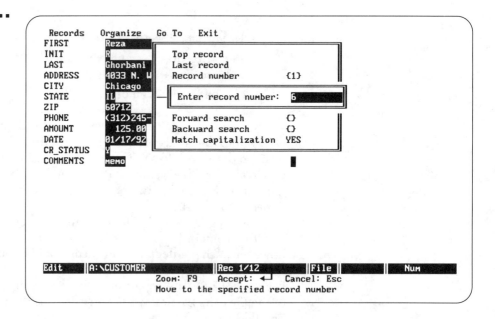

Besides positioning to the beginning and ending location of a file, you can also position directly to a specific record. This assumes, of course, that you know the number of the desired record. For example, suppose that you wish to position to record 6 (the Russell Davis record). This requires the following commands (.GOTO 6):

F10   Invokes the menu bar and the Go To menu.

Record number   Selects the Record number option.

F10   Opens the menu box for the desired record number (Figure 2.7).

Backspace   Erases the current number.

Type 6   Enters the desired record number.

Enter   Displays that record to the screen.

You may also want to move forward or backward within the file a specific number of records at a time. Do this by using the **Skip option** of the Go To menu. Notice that the default entry for the Skip is 10. This means that, if you select this option, you will move forward 10 records at a time. Position the pointer to the top of the file and enter the following commands to skip 3 records at a time:

F10 Invokes the menu bar and the Go To menu.

Skip Selects the Skip option (.SKIP 3).

Enter Executes the command.

Backspace (2) Erases the current contents.

Type 3 Enters the number of records to be skipped.

Enter Executes the command. You should now be at record 4.

You can also go backward within the file by entering a negative number as the skip interval. For example, if you entered −3, you would go backward within the file three records (.SKIP -3).

LOCATING RECORDS USING SEARCH

Positioning to a record when you know the record number is a straightforward task using the Go To menu. What happens, however, when you do not know the record number? In such situations, dBASE commands let you enter the characteristics of the desired record, and dBASE then positions to the record that meets those specifications. In performing this operation, specify the characters you enter for a desired field, and dBASE then compares those with the contents of this field in each record. This search starts with the first record and ends with the last record. To locate a record using this technique, you must know the field to be searched and enter exactly the characters being sought.

Use the Go To option of the menu bar (Figure 2.6) for this operation. Any search starts at the current record and moves forward or backward within the file. The **Forward search option** searches from the current record to the end of the file. The **Backward search option** searches from the current record to the beginning of the file. The **Match capitalization option** ensures that the capitalization in the string being sought matches the specified string. This option can be turned on/off by highlighting the Match capitalization option and pressing Enter.

Before using the search command, position the pointer to the beginning of the file using the following commands:

F10 Invokes the menu bar and the Go To menu.

Top record Selects the Top record option (.GOTO TOP).

Enter Executes the command.

Find the record with the FIRST field contents of Debbie. To initiate a search, the cursor must be in the field that you wish to search (in this search, the cursor is automatically in the FIRST field):

F10 Invokes the menu bar and, if necessary, the Go To menu.

Forward search Selects the Forward search option. The braces

· ·

Figure 2.8

The Forward search criteria box

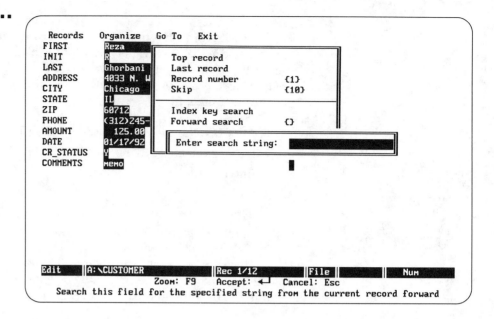

{ } without characters indicate that there is currently no search criteria specified.

Enter   Displays the box for entering the search data (Figure 2.8).

Type Debbie   Enters the search criteria (⸱LOCATE FOR FIRST = "Debbie").

Enter   Executes the command.

In a successful search, the Edit screen reappears, and you are positioned to the record that meets the search criteria. If the search fails, you will receive the error message ✱✱ Not Found ✱✱. To return to Edit, press Esc one or more times.

When specifying search criteria, you can also use the wild cards ✱ and ? in exactly the same fashion as you do in DOS. The ? specifies one position, and the ✱ specifies any remaining characters. For example, if you want to use ✱ for locating any records with the contents of Bloomington in the CITY field, use the following commands:

F10   Invokes the menu bar and the Go To menu.

Top record   Selects the Top record option.

Enter   Executes the command.

Tab (4 times)   Goes to the CITY field.

F10   Invokes the menu bar and the Go To menu.

Forward search   Selects Forward search.

Enter   Executes the command.

Backspace   Erases anything currently in the box.

Type Blo✱   Enters the search criteria.

Enter   Executes the command.

Continuing the Search   Once search criteria have been specified, you can locate other records that meet that criteria by pressing Shift + F4 to go forward in the file and Shift + F3 to go backward. Notice that when you get to the end of the file, dBASE moves the pointer to the beginning of the file and lets you loop through the file again.

The wild card used in conjunction with a substring search does not have a corresponding entry at the dot prompt. If you want to issue such a command, you must use a **String function** ($) for the search. This can be used with a List command. From the dot prompt enter the following command:

```
.LIST FOR "Blo" $CITY
```

```
Record#  FIRST     INIT LAST         ADDRESS                    CITY
STATE ZIP    PHONE          AMOUNT DATE      CR_STATUS COMMENTS
      3  Douglas   C    Acklin      408 E. Monroe              Bloomington
Il    61701 (312)663-8976    55.00 04/01/92 .T.       memo
      5  Arthur    V    Adams       115 Ginger Creek Ct.       Bloomington
Il    61701 (309)828-7290    35.00 03/13/92 .T.       memo
      6  Russell   B    Davis       707 Vale St.               Bloomington
Il    61701 (309)662-1759    35.00 02/27/92 .T.       memo
      7  Debbie    C    Acklin      408 E. Monroe              Bloomington
Il    61701 (309)827-1395    35.00 03/21/92 .T.       memo
     10  Sandy     C    Acklin      408 E. Monroe              Bloomington
Il    61701 (309)829-9901    35.00 02/25/92 .T.       memo
```

You can also use the **Locate** and **Continue commands** from the dot prompt. The Continue command, however, moves only forward in the file, whereas Shift + F3 and Shift + F4 move backward or forward, respectively, within the file. To locate records with Normal in the CITY field requires the following dot commands:

```
. goto top
CUSTOMER: Record No       1
. locate for city = "Normal"
Record =         9
. continue
Record =        11
. continue
End of LOCATE scope
```

Notice that the pointer was moved to the beginning file with the goto top command. The locate command was then entered. dBASE then responded with the record number of the first record meeting the criteria and moved the pointer to that location. If desired, you could use a display command to view that record. The continue command located the next record and moved the pointer to that record. The next continue did not locate a record and generated the End of LOCATE scope message.

ARRANGEMENT COMMANDS

The dBASE package has two commands for rearranging data within a file. The Sort command physically rearranges the contents of a file and creates a new file to hold the rearranged contents. The Index command leaves the original file alone but creates another file to rearrange the record numbers.

SORT

The **Sort command** physically rearranges records according to values contained in one or more specific fields of each record. To do this, the sort does not rearrange the records of the original file but produces a second output file with the contents in a different order.

Before sorting a file, you must first activate it. In using the Sort command, designate the key fields for sorting and name the output file. Unless you state otherwise, this "To file" will have the .DBF extension.

You can specify up to 10 key fields for one sort. Enter the fields in order of importance, the most important first. Separate fields by commas. You cannot sort logical or memo fields.

Unless you choose otherwise, sorts are in ascending order—alphabetically A to Z and numerically 0 to 9. Descending order is the reverse—Z to A and 9 to 0.

 Sort by ZIP Code   In the following example, we will sort the CUSTOMER file in ZIP code order. To do this, first set the default drive to A (or the appropriate drive) and activate the CUSTOMER file and select the Display data option (.SORT ON ZIP TO ZIPCUST). Now follow these steps:

F2   Places the file in tabular format.

F10   Invokes the menu bar.

Organize   Selects the Organize option.

Sort database on field list   Selects Sort database on field list.

Enter   Executes the command.

Shift + F1   Activates a pop-up menu with all field names for the CUSTOMER file (Figure 2.9).

ZIP   Selects the ZIP field.

Enter (4 times)   Executes the command, verifies the ZIP field, verifies ascending order, and accepts the Sort command.

Type ZIPCUST   Names the file to receive the sorted data.

Enter   Executes the sort.

Type SORTED CUSTOMER FILE BY ZIP CODE   Enters the description of the file.

Enter   Finishes storing the file.

Once the sort starts, dBASE displays a box showing how much of the file has been sorted. Once the sort operation is finished, you are returned to the Browse screen. You now have two files: the original CUSTOMER file on disk, which remains unchanged, and the newly created ZIPCUST file, which contains the data from the CUSTOMER file arranged by the contents of the ZIP field. Because you have not changed the activated file, the CUSTOMER file remains active. You can confirm this by simply examining the order of the records on the Browse screen (Figure 2.10).

To verify that you have created the ZIPCUST file properly, press Esc to exit the Browse screen, return to the Control Center, activate the ZIPCUST file (highlight and press Enter), and then select the Display data option and press Enter. You should now see the Browse screen for the ZIPCUST file (Figure 2.11). The records are not in the same order as in the CUSTOMER file but are arranged by the contents of the ZIP field. This means that the record numbers are also different, having been changed to reflect their new locations in the ZIPCUST file.

The process of sorting information by two fields is also straightforward. Suppose you want to sort the CUSTOMER file by name. When two customers

Figure 2.9

The listing of fields activated via the Shift + F1 command

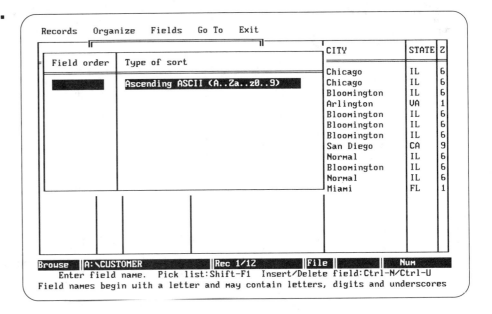

Figure 2.10

The unchanged CUSTOMER file on the Browse screen

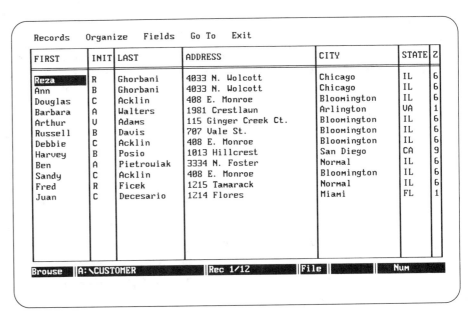

have the same last name, you will want the first names to be in alphabetic order. In this case, the primary sort key (first field specified) is the last name, and the secondary sort key (second field specified) is the first name. Specify your sort fields in the manner previously indicated and place the output in the file ALPHNAME. This requires the dot commands:

`.SORT ON LAST, FIRST TO ALPHNAME`

Using the Control Center requires issuing the following commands:

Esc   Exits the Browse screen for the ZIPCUST file.

CUSTOMER   Selects the CUSTOMER file.

Enter   Executes the command.

Display data   Selects the Display data option.

. . . .

Figure 2.11

The reordered ZIPCUST file on the Browse screen

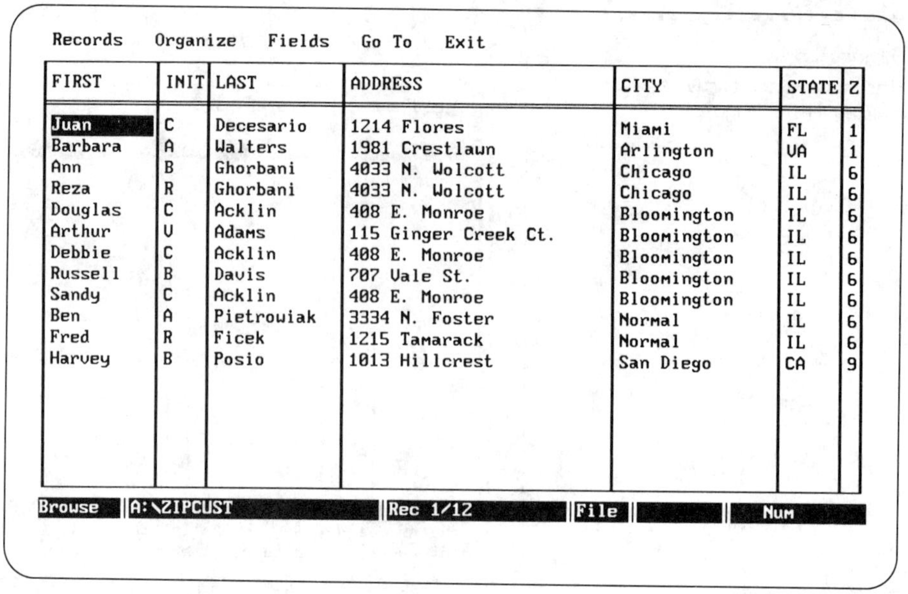

```
Records   Organize   Fields   Go To   Exit

FIRST      INIT LAST      ADDRESS              CITY        STATE Z

Juan       C   Decesario 1214 Flores          Miami       FL    1
Barbara    A   Walters   1981 Crestlaun       Arlington   VA    1
Ann        B   Ghorbani  4033 N. Wolcott      Chicago     IL    6
Reza       R   Ghorbani  4033 N. Wolcott      Chicago     IL    6
Douglas    C   Acklin    408 E. Monroe        Bloomington IL    6
Arthur     V   Adams     115 Ginger Creek Ct. Bloomington IL    6
Debbie     C   Acklin    408 E. Monroe        Bloomington IL    6
Russell    B   Davis     707 Vale St.         Bloomington IL    6
Sandy      C   Acklin    408 E. Monroe        Bloomington IL    6
Ben        A   Pietrowiak 3334 N. Foster      Normal      IL    6
Fred       R   Ficek     1215 Tamarack        Normal      IL    6
Harvey     B   Posio     1013 Hillcrest       San Diego   CA    9




Browse    A:\ZIPCUST              Rec 1/12      File              Num
```

Enter   Executes the command.

F10   Invokes the menu bar.

Organize   Selects the Organize option.

Sort database on field list   Selects Sort database on field list.

Enter   Executes the command.

Shift + F1   Lists the fields of the CUSTOMER file.

LAST   Selects the LAST field.

Enter (3 times)   Executes the command, verifies the LAST field, and verifies the LAST field as the primary sort, displays the next field box, and signifies the last field.

Shift + F1   Lists the fields of the CUSTOMER file.

FIRST   Selects the FIRST field.

Enter (4 times)   Executes the command, verifies the FIRST field.

Type ALPHNAME   Names the output file.

Enter   Specifies the name of the output file.

Type CUSTOMER FILE IN ALPHABETIC ORDER   Enters the description of the new file.

Enter   Specifies the name of the input file.

To verify that you have created the ALPHNAME file properly, press Esc to exit the Browse screen, return to the Control Center, activate the ALPHNAME file (highlight and press Enter), and then select the Display data option and press Enter. You should now see the Browse screen for the ALPHNAME file (Figure 2.12). The records are not in the same order as in the CUSTOMER file but are arranged in order by name.

Using the Sort command is not usually the best way to arrange data within a file. Several restrictions apply to it:

1. It usually takes a lot of computer time. Although this is not evident with a small file such as CUSTOMER, an attempt to use Sort on a file containing 3,000 records would make it obvious.

Figure 2.12

The reordered ALPHNAME file

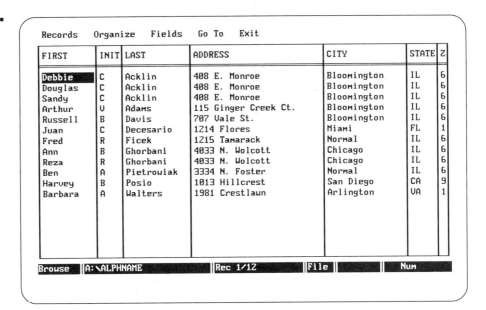

FIRST	INIT	LAST	ADDRESS	CITY	STATE	Z
Debbie	C	Acklin	408 E. Monroe	Bloomington	IL	6
Douglas	C	Acklin	408 E. Monroe	Bloomington	IL	6
Sandy	C	Acklin	408 E. Monroe	Bloomington	IL	6
Arthur	V	Adams	115 Ginger Creek Ct.	Bloomington	IL	6
Russell	B	Davis	707 Vale St.	Bloomington	IL	6
Juan	C	Decesario	1214 Flores	Miami	FL	1
Fred	R	Ficek	1215 Tamarack	Normal	IL	6
Ann	B	Ghorbani	4033 N. Wolcott	Chicago	IL	6
Reza	R	Ghorbani	4033 N. Wolcott	Chicago	IL	6
Ben	A	Pietrowiak	3334 N. Foster	Normal	IL	6
Harvey	B	Posio	1013 Hillcrest	San Diego	CA	9
Barbara	A	Walters	1981 Crestlawn	Arlington	VA	1

Browse   A:\ALPHNAME   Rec 1/12   File   Num

2. The Sort command creates a new file every time it is executed. This takes up much disk storage when you sort large files.

3. The record numbers change from one file to another.

INDEX

The best way to reorder records is to use the **Index command**, which does not rearrange them physically but reorders them logically, without moving records. This is accomplished by an index file in which each specified field points to the appropriate record in the specified file. The contents of the original file remain unchanged, with the same physical file order and the same record numbers; the new index file holds the logical order of the file.

Single-Field Indexes   A **single-field index** file is ordered by the contents of one field only.

To prepare for the following examples, activate the CUSTOMER file and create a ZIP code index (. INDEX ON ZIP TAG ZIP). From the Control Center, issue the following commands:

F2   Places the file in tabular form.

F10   Invokes the menu bar.

Organize   Selects the Organize option.

Create new index   Selects the Create new index option.

Enter   Displays the index definition box (Figure 2.13).

Enter   Opens the Name of index option.

Type ZIP   Names the index.

Enter (twice)   Executes the command and activates the Index expression entry.

Type ZIP   Names the field that is to be used to create the index.

Enter   Executes the command.

Ctrl + End   Creates the index.

Figure 2.13

The index definition box

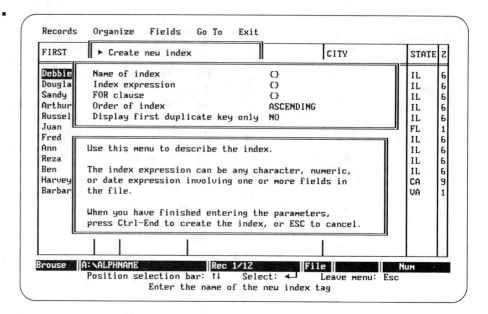

```
  Records   Organize   Fields   Go To   Exit

 ┌─FIRST──────┬► Create new index ─────────────────────────╥─────┬CITY──────┬STATE┬Z┐
 │            │                                             ║     │          │     │ │
 │ Debbie     │  Name of index                    {}        ║     │          │ IL  │6│
 │ Dougla     │  Index expression                 {}        ║     │          │ IL  │6│
 │ Sandy      │  FOR clause                       {}        ║     │          │ IL  │6│
 │ Arthur     │  Order of index                   ASCENDING ║     │          │ IL  │6│
 │ Russel     │  Display first duplicate key only NO        ║     │          │ IL  │6│
 │ Juan       └─────────────────────────────────────────────╜     │          │ FL  │1│
 │ Fred       ┌───────────────────────────────────────────────┐   │          │ IL  │6│
 │ Ann        │  Use this menu to describe the index.         │   │          │ IL  │6│
 │ Reza       │                                               │   │          │ IL  │6│
 │ Ben        │  The index expression can be any character, numeric, │   │   │ IL  │6│
 │ Harvey     │  or date expression involving one or more fields in  │   │   │ CA  │9│
 │ Barbar     │  the file.                                    │   │          │ VA  │1│
 │            │                                               │   │          │     │ │
 │            │  When you have finished entering the parameters,     │   │          │ │
 │            │  press Ctrl-End to create the index, or ESC to cancel.│  │          │ │
 │            └───────────────────────────────────────────────┘   │          │     │ │
 │            │        │        │        │        │              │          │     │ │
 ├Browse──┬A:\ALPHNAME────────────────────┬Rec 1/12────┬File─┬──────┬Num─────┤
              Position selection bar: ↑↓    Select: ↵    Leave menu: Esc
                          Enter the name of the new index tag
```

Figure 2.14

The Browse screen showing the CUS-
TOMER file in order by the ZIP index

```
  Records   Organize   Fields   Go To   Exit

 ┌FIRST─────┬INIT┬LAST──────┬ADDRESS────────────┬CITY────────┬STATE┬Z┐
 │ Juan     │ C  │ Decesario│ 1214 Flores        │ Miami      │ FL  │1│
 │ Barbara  │ A  │ Walters   │ 1981 Crestlawn     │ Arlington  │ VA  │1│
 │ Reza     │ R  │ Ghorbani  │ 4033 N. Wolcott    │ Chicago    │ IL  │6│
 │ Ann      │ B  │ Ghorbani  │ 4033 N. Wolcott    │ Chicago    │ IL  │6│
 │ Douglas  │ C  │ Acklin    │ 408 E. Monroe      │ Bloomington│ IL  │6│
 │ Arthur   │ V  │ Adams     │ 115 Ginger Creek Ct.│ Bloomington│ IL │6│
 │ Russell  │ B  │ Davis     │ 707 Vale St.       │ Bloomington│ IL  │6│
 │ Debbie   │ C  │ Acklin    │ 408 E. Monroe      │ Bloomington│ IL  │6│
 │ Sandy    │ C  │ Acklin    │ 408 E. Monroe      │ Bloomington│ IL  │6│
 │ Ben      │ A  │ Pietrowiak│ 3334 N. Foster     │ Normal     │ IL  │6│
 │ Fred     │ R  │ Ficek     │ 1215 Tamarack      │ Normal     │ IL  │6│
 │ Harvey   │ B  │ Posio     │ 1013 Hillcrest     │ San Diego  │ CA  │9│
 │          │    │           │                    │            │     │ │
 ├Browse──┬A:\CUSTOMER──────────────────┬Rec 12/12───┬File─┬──────┬Num─────┤
```

Zip Code	Record Number
12562	00012
13411	00004
60712	00001
60712	00002
61701	00003
61701	00005
61701	00006
61701	00007
61701	00010
61761	00009
61761	00011
94307	00008

Figure 2.15

Information contained in the ZIP index
file: the ZIP code and the location of
each record

Once the Ctrl + End command is issued, a message box appears and tells
you what percentage of the file is currently indexed. Once the index is created,
the file is automatically displayed on the Browse screen in the index order
(Figure 2.14). Press Enter several times to get the ZIP code column displayed
on the Browse screen.

The above steps have resulted in the creating of an index file called ZIP;
each record in the ZIP index contains the ZIP field for a record in the CUS-
TOMER file and the number of the record with that particular ZIP code value
(Figure 2.15). When the records are displayed, dBASE first accesses the ZIP
index file, which in turn prints the appropriate record from the CUSTOMER
file.

When dBASE lists the records from an indexed file, it performs a number
of tasks automatically. First, it goes to the ZIP index (see Figure 2.15) and
finds ZIP 12562. It also finds that record 12 of the CUSTOMER file holds the
data for this index entry. dBASE now accesses record 12 of the CUSTOMER

file. It then moves to the second index entry and repeats the process until all index entries have been processed.

Because an index only contains the data from the specified field, it is a small file that can be loaded into RAM and can be searched quickly to locate records. Up to 10 indexes can be in use simultaneously, but only the first index specified can be used to actually locate records. Whenever a change is made to a field that is used in an index or when records are added or deleted, the indexes are automatically updated by dBASE to reflect the changes. Working with several indexes open and a large database can result in a slower response for the user and can, as a result, slow editing operations. This is a small price to pay for the flexibility provided by indexing.

As you can see in this example, as soon as the index is built, the file is redisplayed using that index order. If you leave dBASE or create another index and then want to redisplay the file in the prior index order, you must issue the following commands after the file is invoked (SET ORDER TO ZIP):

F10   Invokes the menu bar.

Organize   Selects the Organize option.

Order records by index   Selects Order records by index.

Enter   Displays listing of the index files on disk.

ZIP   Selects the ZIP entry.

Enter   Activates the ZIP index. The file is now displayed in the index order.

HINTS/HAZARDS

The dBASE IV package has two types of index files that it uses to keep track of indexes for a file. The first is the .MDX production multiple-index file that dBASE IV automatically maintains for any index created using the Control Center. The second is the .NDX file created for any index generated at the dot prompt without the TAG entry. Because the advantages of using the multiple index far outweigh creating individual indexes for a file, only the multiple-index method is covered in this text.

The production multiple-index file (.MDX) is automatically created for any database file created using dBASE IV. It can store information about 47 different indexes for that file. When you are using dBASE IV from the Control Center, any indexes created are immediately added as an entry to, in this case, the CUSTOMER.MDX file, using the automatic TAG command. As the index is created, you can see the box displaying the following message: .INDEX ON ZIP TAG ZIP. The message Master Index: Zip now appears on the screen.

If you wish to use the CUSTOMER file via the ZIP index order tag from the dot prompt, enter the following commands:

```
.USE CUSTOMER
.SET ORDER TO ZIP
```

Anytime that you now wish to access the file in a different order, you must issue a new Set Order To command and specify the name of the new tag.

The advantage of using the multiple-index method is that dBASE IV keeps track of all of the index entries that have been created and automatically updates them when changes have been made to a record field that is used in an index tag.

Figure 2.16

The CUSTOMER file on the Browse screen in last name order

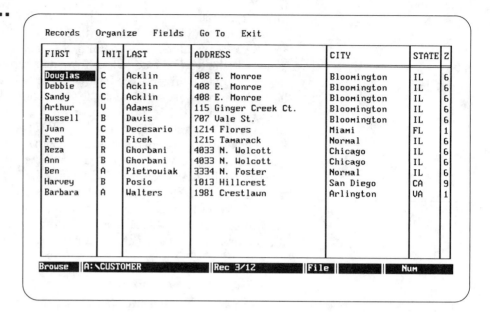

	Records	Organize	Fields	Go To	Exit		
FIRST	INIT	LAST	ADDRESS		CITY	STATE	Z
Douglas	C	Acklin	408 E. Monroe		Bloomington	IL	6
Debbie	C	Acklin	408 E. Monroe		Bloomington	IL	6
Sandy	C	Acklin	408 E. Monroe		Bloomington	IL	6
Arthur	V	Adams	115 Ginger Creek Ct.		Bloomington	IL	6
Russell	B	Davis	707 Vale St.		Bloomington	IL	6
Juan	C	Decesario	1214 Flores		Miami	FL	1
Fred	R	Ficek	1215 Tamarack		Normal	IL	6
Reza	R	Ghorbani	4033 N. Wolcott		Chicago	IL	6
Ann	B	Ghorbani	4033 N. Wolcott		Chicago	IL	6
Ben	A	Pietrowiak	3334 N. Foster		Normal	IL	6
Harvey	B	Posio	1013 Hillcrest		San Diego	CA	9
Barbara	A	Walters	1981 Crestlawn		Arlington	VA	1

`Browse  A:\CUSTOMER          Rec 3/12      File        Num`

Create an index using the LAST field (.INDEX ON LAST TAG LAST). The following example creates an index LAST from the contents of the LAST field of the CUSTOMER file:

F10   Invokes the menu bar.

Organize   Selects the Organize option.

Create new index   Selects the Create new index option.

Enter (twice)   Executes the command and opens the Name of index option.

Type LAST   Names the index.

Enter (twice)   Executes the command and opens the Index expression box.

Type LAST   Names the field to be used in creating the index.

Enter   Executes the command.

Ctrl + End   Builds the index. The Browse screen now displays the contents of the CUSTOMER file in order by last name (Figure 2.16).

Multiple-Field Indexes   What if you want the file to appear in order by more than one field, for example, by first name and last name field contents? The Index command manages this task easily by letting you **concatenate** (join) fields in creating the index. The result is a **multiple-field index**. The first multiple-field index here will arrange the file alphabetically first name within last name.

To create the LFNAME index (.INDEX ON LAST + FIRST TAG LFNAME), with the CUSTOMER file activated (it already is unless you have just started dBASE), issue the following commands:

F10   Invokes the menu bar.

Organize   Selects the Organize option.

Create new index   Selects the Create new index option.

Enter (twice)   Executes the command and opens the Name of index option.

Figure 2.17

The screen used to concatenate files for creating the LFNAME index file

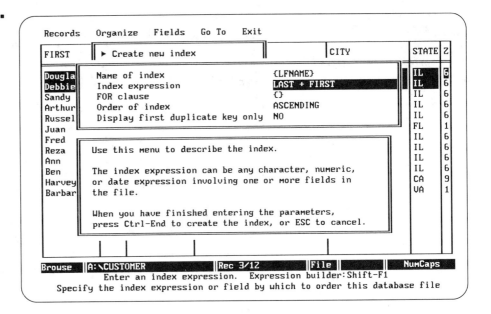

Figure 2.18

The Browse screen with the CUS-TOMER in alphabetic order via the LFNAME index

```
 Records   Organize   Fields   Go To   Exit
┌─────────┬────┬──────────┬────────────────────┬───────────┬─────┬─┐
│ FIRST   │INIT│LAST      │ADDRESS             │CITY       │STATE│Z│
├─────────┼────┼──────────┼────────────────────┼───────────┼─────┼─┤
│ Debbie  │ C  │Acklin    │408 E. Monroe       │Bloomington│ IL  │6│
│ Douglas │ C  │Acklin    │408 E. Monroe       │Bloomington│ IL  │6│
│ Sandy   │ C  │Acklin    │408 E. Monroe       │Bloomington│ IL  │6│
│ Arthur  │ V  │Adams     │115 Ginger Creek Ct.│Bloomington│ IL  │6│
│ Russell │ B  │Davis     │707 Vale St.        │Bloomington│ IL  │6│
│ Juan    │ C  │Decesario │1214 Flores         │Miami      │ FL  │1│
│ Fred    │ R  │Ficek     │1215 Tamarack       │Normal     │ IL  │6│
│ Ann     │ B  │Ghorbani  │4033 N. Wolcott     │Chicago    │ IL  │6│
│ Reza    │ R  │Ghorbani  │4033 N. Wolcott     │Chicago    │ IL  │6│
│ Ben     │ A  │Pietrowiak│3334 N. Foster      │Normal     │ IL  │6│
│ Harvey  │ B  │Posio     │1013 Hillcrest      │San Diego  │ CA  │9│
│ Barbara │ A  │Walters   │1981 Crestlawn      │Arlington  │ VA  │1│
│         │    │          │                    │           │     │ │
│         │    │          │                    │           │     │ │
│         │    │          │                    │           │     │ │
│         │    │          │                    │           │     │ │
└─────────┴────┴──────────┴────────────────────┴───────────┴─────┴─┘
 Browse   A:\CUSTOMER              Rec 7/12       File          NumCaps
```

Type LFNAME   Names the index.

Enter (twice)   Executes the command and opens the `Index expression` entry.

Type LAST + FIRST   Enters the fields to be used in the index (Figure 2.17).

Enter   Executes the command.

Ctrl + End   Builds the index. The Browse screen now displays the CUSTOMER file in alphabetic order via the LFNAME index (Figure 2.18).

Within the last name order, the Acklin and the Ghorbani records are now listed in alphabetic order by first name.

Figure 2.19

The Browse screen with the CUS-
TOMER in order via the ZIPLFNAM
index

Records	Organize	Fields	Go To	Exit

FIRST	INIT	LAST	ADDRESS	CITY	STATE	Z
Juan	C	Decesario	1214 Flores	Miami	FL	1
Barbara	A	Walters	1981 Crestlaun	Arlington	VA	1
Ann	B	Ghorbani	4033 N. Wolcott	Chicago	IL	6
Reza	R	Ghorbani	4033 N. Wolcott	Chicago	IL	6
Debbie	C	Acklin	408 E. Monroe	Bloomington	IL	6
Douglas	C	Acklin	408 E. Monroe	Bloomington	IL	6
Sandy	C	Acklin	408 E. Monroe	Bloomington	IL	6
Arthur	V	Adams	115 Ginger Creek Ct.	Bloomington	IL	6
Russell	B	Davis	707 Vale St.	Bloomington	IL	6
Fred	R	Ficek	1215 Tamarack	Normal	IL	6
Ben	A	Pietrowiak	3334 N. Foster	Normal	IL	6
Harvey	B	Posio	1013 Hillcrest	San Diego	CA	9

Browse	A:\CUSTOMER	Rec 12/12	File	NumCaps

To create the ZIPLFNAM index (. INDEX ON ZIP + LAST + FIRST
TAG ZIPLFNAM), the following commands extend the index order to three
fields and generate a display of the file in order by ZIP code, last name, and
first name:

F10   Invokes the menu bar.

Organize   Selects the Organize option.

Create new index   Selects the Create new index option.

Enter (twice)   Executes the command and opens the Index
expression option.

Type ZIPLFNAM   Names the index.

Enter (twice)   Executes the command and opens the Index
expression entry.

Type ZIP + LAST + FIRST   Names the fields to be used in the
index.

Enter   Executes the command.

Ctrl + End   Builds the index. The Browse screen now displays the
contents of the CUSTOMER file in alphabetic order via the ZIPLFNAM
index (Figure 2.19).

Indexing by Numeric Order   You can also index data in numeric order. If
the created index refers only to one field in the original file, and that field is
numeric, use the same procedure for creating any other single-field index.
However, the data in an index file are always stored as character data.

When an index refers to several numeric or numeric and character data
fields, the Index command will operate only on character data. To create a
multiple-field, **mixed-data index**, you must change the numeric fields in the
original file to character data.

The following example creates an index ordered by the AMOUNT field
only (. INDEX ON AMOUNT TAG AMOUNT). The file then appears in order
by the AMOUNT field. Keep in mind that the index entry is now character
data, whereas the data in the original file remain numeric.

Figure 2.20

The Browse screen with the CUS-TOMER in order via the AMOUNT index

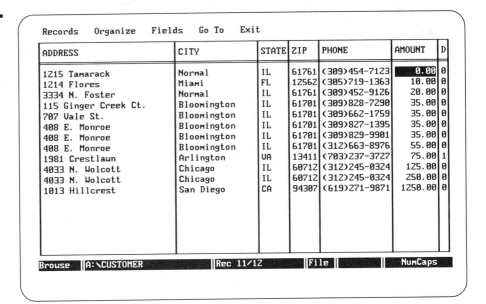

Records Organize Fields Go To Exit						
ADDRESS	CITY	STATE	ZIP	PHONE	AMOUNT	D
1215 Tamarack	Normal	IL	61761	(309)454-7123	0.00	0
1214 Flores	Miami	FL	12562	(305)719-1363	10.00	0
3334 N. Foster	Normal	IL	61761	(309)452-9126	20.00	0
115 Ginger Creek Ct.	Bloomington	IL	61701	(309)828-7290	35.00	0
707 Vale St.	Bloomington	IL	61701	(309)662-1759	35.00	0
408 E. Monroe	Bloomington	IL	61701	(309)827-1395	35.00	0
408 E. Monroe	Bloomington	IL	61701	(309)829-9901	35.00	0
408 E. Monroe	Bloomington	IL	61701	(312)663-8976	55.00	0
1981 Crestlaun	Arlington	VA	13411	(703)237-3727	75.00	1
4033 N. Wolcott	Chicago	IL	60712	(312)245-0324	125.00	0
4033 N. Wolcott	Chicago	IL	60712	(312)245-0324	250.00	0
1013 Hillcrest	San Diego	CA	94307	(619)271-9871	1250.00	0

Browse	A:\CUSTOMER	Rec 11/12	File	NumCaps

F10 Invokes the menu bar.

Organize Selects the Organize option.

Create new index Selects the Create new index option.

Enter (twice) Executes the command and opens the Name of index option.

Type AMOUNT Names the index.

Enter (twice) Executes the command and opens the Index expression entry.

Type AMOUNT Names the field to be used in the index.

Enter Executes the command.

Ctrl + End Builds the index. The Browse screen now displays the contents of the CUSTOMER file in order via the AMOUNT index (Figure 2.20).

Creating a mixed-data, multiple-field index with a numeric field requires the use of the STR (string) function; otherwise, the screen displays an error message. The ZIPAMOUN index contains the ZIP and AMOUNT fields and is created using the following instructions (.INDEX ON ZIP + STR(AMOUNT,8,2) TAG ZIPAMOUN):

F10 Invokes the menu bar.

Organize Selects the Organize option.

Create new index Selects the Create new index option.

Enter (twice) Executes the command and opens the Name of index option.

Type ZIPAMOUN Names the index.

Enter (twice) Executes the command and opens the Index expression entry.

Type ZIP + AMOUNT Names the field to be used in the index.

Enter Executes the command. The screen displays an error message indicating that there is a data-type mismatch (Figure 2.21).

••••••••••••••••••••

Figure 2.21

The data-type mismatch error message

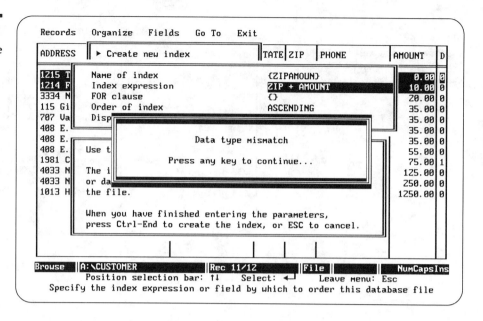

```
 Records   Organize   Fields   Go To   Exit

 ADDRESS      ┃  ▶ Create new index            ┃TATE┃ZIP┃ PHONE       ┃ AMOUNT ┃D┃

 1215 T     ┃   Name of index        {ZIPAMOUN}      ┃         0.00 ┃0┃
 1214 F     ┃   Index expression     ZIP + AMOUNT    ┃        10.00 ┃0┃
 3334 N     ┃   FOR clause           {}              ┃        20.00 ┃0┃
 115 Gi     ┃   Order of index       ASCENDING       ┃        35.00 ┃0┃
 707 Va     ┃   Disp                                 ┃        35.00 ┃0┃
 408 E.     ┃        ┌──────────────────────────────┐┃        35.00 ┃0┃
 408 E.     ┃   Use t│    Data type mismatch         │┃        55.00 ┃0┃
 1981 C     ┃        │                               │┃        75.00 ┃1┃
 4033 N     ┃   The i│    Press any key to continue...│┃       125.00 ┃0┃
 4033 N     ┃   or da└──────────────────────────────┘┃       250.00 ┃0┃
 1013 H     ┃   the file.                             ┃      1250.00 ┃0┃
            ┃                                         ┃
            ┃   When you have finished entering the parameters,
            ┃   press Ctrl-End to create the index, or ESC to cancel.

 Browse  ┃A:\CUSTOMER        ┃Rec 11/12    ┃ ┃File┃ ┃        NumCapsIns
          Position selection bar: ↑↓   Select: ↵    Leave menu: Esc
    Specify the index expression or field by which to order this database file
```

••••••••••••••••••••

Figure 2.22

The Browse screen with the CUS-TOMER in order via the ZIPAMOUN index

```
 Records   Organize   Fields   Go To   Exit

 ADDRESS            ┃ CITY        ┃STATE┃ZIP  ┃ PHONE        ┃ AMOUNT ┃D┃

 1214 Flores        ┃ Miami       ┃ FL  ┃12562┃(305)719-1363 ┃  10.00 ┃0┃
 1981 Crestlaun     ┃ Arlington   ┃ VA  ┃13411┃(703)237-3727 ┃  75.00 ┃1┃
 4033 N. Wolcott    ┃ Chicago     ┃ IL  ┃60712┃(312)245-0324 ┃ 125.00 ┃0┃
 4033 N. Wolcott    ┃ Chicago     ┃ IL  ┃60712┃(312)245-0324 ┃ 250.00 ┃0┃
 115 Ginger Creek Ct.┃ Bloomington ┃ IL  ┃61701┃(309)828-7290 ┃  35.00 ┃0┃
 707 Vale St.       ┃ Bloomington ┃ IL  ┃61701┃(309)662-1759 ┃  35.00 ┃0┃
 408 E. Monroe      ┃ Bloomington ┃ IL  ┃61701┃(309)827-1395 ┃  35.00 ┃0┃
 408 E. Monroe      ┃ Bloomington ┃ IL  ┃61701┃(309)829-9901 ┃  35.00 ┃0┃
 408 E. Monroe      ┃ Bloomington ┃ IL  ┃61701┃(312)663-8976 ┃  55.00 ┃0┃
 1215 Tamarack      ┃ Normal      ┃ IL  ┃61761┃(309)454-7123 ┃   0.00 ┃0┃
 3334 N. Foster     ┃ Normal      ┃ IL  ┃61761┃(309)452-9126 ┃  20.00 ┃0┃
 1013 Hillcrest     ┃ San Diego   ┃ CA  ┃94307┃(619)271-9871 ┃1250.00 ┃0┃

 Browse  ┃A:\CUSTOMER        ┃Rec 12/12    ┃ ┃File┃ ┃        NumCaps
```

Enter (twice)   Clears the error message and reactivates the I n d e x e x p r e s s i o n box.

Type ZIP + STR(AMOUNT,8,2)   Enters the new field specification. The 8 indicates that the field is eight positions wide, and the 2 indicates that there are two positions to the right of the decimal.

Enter   Executes the command.

Ctrl + End   Builds the index. The Browse screen now displays the contents of the CUSTOMER file in order via the ZIPAMOUN index (Figure 2.22).

Limiting the Index Size   If you have an extremely large file, you may not want to include all records in an index. For example, assume that you are only interested in those records for Bloomington, IL (ZIP = 61701) and you want to display and manipulate only those records. Do this by using the FOR condition in the index.

Figure 2.23

The Browse screen with the CUS-
TOMER in order via the ZLFNAME
index

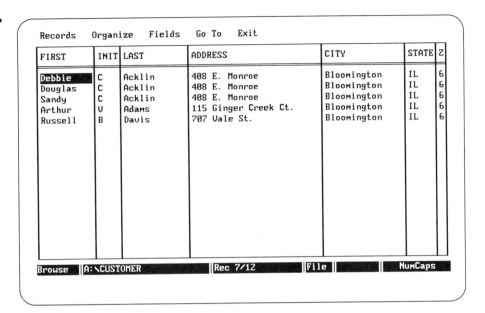

FIRST	INIT	LAST	ADDRESS	CITY	STATE	Z
Debbie	C	Acklin	408 E. Monroe	Bloomington	IL	6
Douglas	C	Acklin	408 E. Monroe	Bloomington	IL	6
Sandy	C	Acklin	408 E. Monroe	Bloomington	IL	6
Arthur	V	Adams	115 Ginger Creek Ct.	Bloomington	IL	6
Russell	B	Davis	707 Vale St.	Bloomington	IL	6

Records   Organize   Fields   Go To   Exit

Browse   A:\CUSTOMER   Rec 7/12   File   NumCaps

    This example creates an alphabetic listing of the CUSTOMER file but only
includes those records with 61701 in the index. Use the following commands
to create the index ZLFNAME (.INDEX ON LAST + FIRST TAG
ZLFNAME FOR ZIP = '61701'):

F10   Invokes the menu bar.

Organize   Selects the Organize option.

Create new index   Selects the Create new index option.

Enter (twice)   Executes the command and opens the Name of
index option.

Type ZLFNAME   Names the index.

Enter (twice)   Executes the command and opens the Index
expression entry.

Type LAST + FIRST   Enters the fields to be used in the index.

Enter (twice)   Executes the command and opens the FOR clause
box.

Type ZIP = '61701'   Enters the condition criteria.

Enter   Executes the command.

Ctrl + End   Builds the index. The Browse screen now displays the
contents of the CUSTOMER file in order via the ZLFNAME index
(Figure 2.23). Notice that there are only the five records displayed that
have a ZIP code of 61701.

Deleting Unwanted Indexes   As you are creating indexes, you may find
that you have indexes on disk that are no longer needed. Such indexes can be
deleted by using the Remove unwanted indexes option from the Organize
menu.

The following example removes the ZLFNAME (.DELETE TAG
ZLFNAME):

F10   Invokes the menu bar.

Organize   Selects the Organize option.

Remove unwanted index tag   Selects Remove unwanted
indexes.

Enter   Executes the command. A series of boxes appears showing the
indexes and the fields used to create it (Figure 2.24).

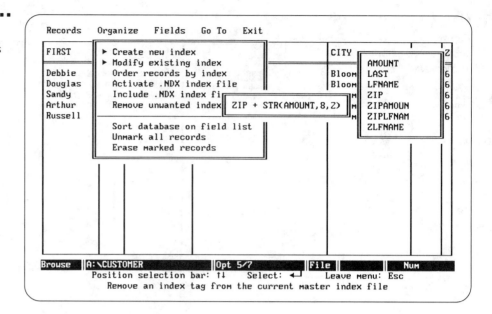

Figure 2.24

The screen containing the index files that can be deleted

ZLFNAME   Selects the ZLFNAME index.

Enter   Executes the command.

HINTS/HAZARDS

Save several keystrokes when you invoke the menu bar to select a menu option. Instead of pressing F10 followed by Arrow keys to highlight the desired menu option, issue an Alt command followed by the first character of the desired option.

LOCATING RECORDS IN AN INDEXED FILE

You have already been introduced to various commands that allow you to locate records in an unordered file: Locate, Go To, and Skip. The **Seek command** can only access an indexed file. Both the file and the index must be referenced in a Use statement from the dot prompt or activated using the Control Center.

The Seek command uses the index to find any records that match the search criteria. Because the information in the index is all character data, enter the search criteria inside quotation marks if you are using the dot prompt. This is not necessary if you are using the Control Center.

Seek with the ZIP Index   The following example assumes that the CUSTOMER file has been invoked (.SET ORDER TO ZIP) and uses the ZIP index to locate records: (.SEEK '61761').

F10   Invokes the menu bar.

Organize   Selects the Organize option.

Order records by index   Selects Order records by index.

Enter   Displays a listing of the .NDX files on disk.

ZIP   Selects the ZIP entry.

Enter   Activates the ZIP index. The Browse screen now displays the file in the ZIP index order.

Figure 2.25

The entry box for the Seek criteria

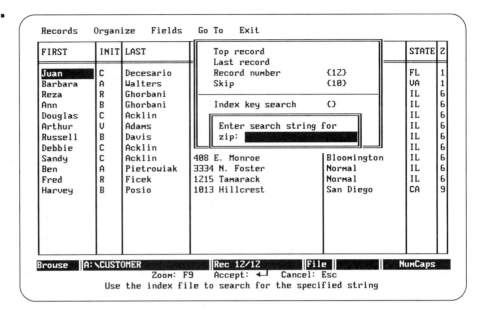

```
Records    Organize    Fields    Go To    Exit

FIRST     INIT LAST              Top record                      STATE Z
                                 Last record
Juan      C    Decesario         Record number      {12}         FL    1
Barbara   A    Walters           Skip               {10}         VA    1
Reza      R    Ghorbani                                          IL    6
Ann       B    Ghorbani          Index key search   {}          IL    6
Douglas   C    Acklin                                            IL    6
Arthur    V    Adams             Enter search string for         IL    6
Russell   B    Davis             zip:                            IL    6
Debbie    C    Acklin                                            IL    6
Sandy     C    Acklin     408 E. Monroe        Bloomington       IL    6
Ben       A    Pietrowiak 3334 N. Foster       Normal            IL    6
Fred      R    Ficek      1215 Tamarack        Normal            IL    6
Harvey    B    Posio      1013 Hillcrest       San Diego         CA    9




Browse  A:\CUSTOMER          Rec 12/12      File            NumCaps
              Zoom: F9    Accept: ↵    Cancel: Esc
        Use the index file to search for the specified string
```

Figure 2.26

The Browse screen with the records containing the ZIP code 61761 after the Seek command has executed

```
Records    Organize    Fields    Go To    Exit

ADDRESS                  CITY          STATE ZIP   PHONE          AMOUNT   D

1013 Hillcrest           San Diego     CA    94307 (619)271-9871  1250.00 0










Browse  A:\CUSTOMER          Rec 8/12       File            Num    Ins
```

F10   Invokes the menu bar.

Go To   Selects the Go To entry.

Index key search   Selects Index key search.

Enter   Displays the entry box (Figure 2.25).

Type 94307   Enters the search criteria.

Enter   Displays to the screen the records that meet that criteria (Figure 2.26).

The Seek command directs dBASE to place the pointer at the first occurrence of the 61761 ZIP code in the ZIP index. Unless the ** Not Found ** error message is displayed, dBASE positions the pointer at that record location and displays those records that meet the criteria.

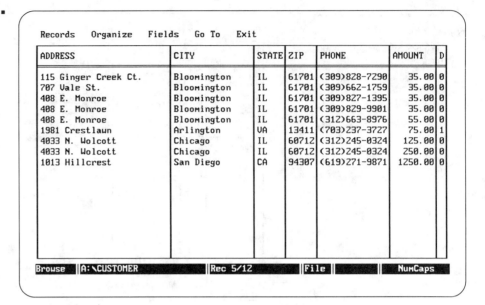

```
  Records   Organize   Fields   Go To   Exit

 ADDRESS                CITY          STATE ZIP   PHONE           AMOUNT   D

 115 Ginger Creek Ct.   Bloomington   IL    61701 (309)828-7290     35.00 0
 707 Vale St.           Bloomington   IL    61701 (309)662-1759     35.00 0
 408 E. Monroe          Bloomington   IL    61701 (309)827-1395     35.00 0
 408 E. Monroe          Bloomington   IL    61701 (309)829-9901     35.00 0
 408 E. Monroe          Bloomington   IL    61701 (312)663-8976     55.00 0
 1981 Crestlawn         Arlington     VA    13411 (703)237-3727     75.00 1
 4033 N. Wolcott        Chicago       IL    60712 (312)245-0324    125.00 0
 4033 N. Wolcott        Chicago       IL    60712 (312)245-0324    250.00 0
 1013 Hillcrest         San Diego     CA    94307 (619)271-9871   1250.00 0

 Browse    A:\CUSTOMER             Rec 5/12      File          NumCaps
```

Seek with the AMOUNT Index   The following example assumes that the CUSTOMER file has been invoked (.SET ORDER TO AMOUNT) (.SEEK 35.00) and uses the AMOUNT index to locate records:

F10   Invokes the menu bar.

Organize   Selects the Organize option.

Order records by index   Selects Order records by index.

Enter   Displays a listing of the .NDX files on disk.

AMOUNT   Selects the AMOUNT entry.

Enter   Activates the AMOUNT index. The screen now displays the file in the AMOUNT index order.

F10   Invokes the menu bar.

Go To   Selects the Go To entry.

Index key search   Selects the Index key search.

Enter   Displays the entry box.

Backspace   Deletes the prior contents.

Type 35.00   Enters the search criteria.

Enter   Executes the command. The screen now displays the records that meet that criteria (Figure 2.27).

Notice that records with amounts other than 35.00 appear on your screen (Figure 2.27). The first entries match exactly, and the other entries have one or several characters that match. This occurs because dBASE positions the pointer to the first record that matches the Seek criteria and then displays the remaining records.

Seek with the LAST Index   The following example assumes that the CUSTOMER file has been invoked (.SET ORDER TO LAST) (.SEEK 'Ghorbani') and uses the LAST index to locate records:

Figure 2.28

The Browse screen with the records after records for the LAST index are located

```
 Records    Organize    Fields    Go To    Exit
┌──────────┬────┬──────────┬───────────────┬──────────┬─────┬─┐
│FIRST     │INIT│LAST      │ADDRESS        │CITY      │STATE│Z│
├──────────┼────┼──────────┼───────────────┼──────────┼─────┼─┤
│Reza      │R   │Ghorbani  │4033 N. Wolcott│Chicago   │IL   │6│
│Ann       │B   │Ghorbani  │4033 N. Wolcott│Chicago   │IL   │6│
│Ben       │A   │Pietrowiak│3334 N. Foster │Normal    │IL   │6│
│Harvey    │B   │Posio     │1013 Hillcrest │San Diego │CA   │9│
│Barbara   │A   │Walters   │1981 Crestlawn │Arlington │VA   │1│
│          │    │          │               │          │     │ │
└──────────┴────┴──────────┴───────────────┴──────────┴─────┴─┘
 Browse   A:\CUSTOMER              Rec 1/12        File          Num   Ins
```

F10   Invokes the menu bar.

Organize   Selects the Organize option.

Order records by index   Selects Order records by index.

Enter   Displays a listing of the .NDX files on disk.

LAST   Selects the LAST entry.

Enter   Activates the LAST index and displays the file in the LAST index order.

F10   Invokes the menu bar.

Go To   Selects the Go To entry.

Index key search   Selects the Index key search.

Enter   Displays the entry box.

Backspace   Erases the prior contents.

Type Ghorbani   Enters the search criteria.

Enter   Executes the command and displays the records that meet that criteria (Figure 2.28).

CHAPTER REVIEW

The Browse command displays and changes records in a file. Browse differs from Edit because it can display multiple records to the screen at one time. It also lets you specify the fields to be displayed if it is entered from the dot prompt. By using the Browse command, you can quickly move through the file in an index file order and manually make changes to selected records.

The Go To menu provides a number of ways to position the pointer using dBASE. It also lets you search both ordered and unordered files.

The dBASE IV package provides two ways to order records within a file: the Sort command and the Index command. The Sort command creates files in which the records are sorted by one or more specified fields. For large files, it is time-consuming.

The Index command creates an index whose contents consist of the key field of each record and the location of each record on disk. The data file is left in its original order, whereas the index is arranged in the desired order. To access a record, dBASE first goes to the index file to find the location of the desired record and then goes to the identified location in the data file. An index file can be built using a number of fields and will produce the information in only one pass. For example, the file could be logically arranged in last name/first name order with only one statement. The term *logically* emphasizes that the original file remains in its original order; only the index file is arranged to reflect the changed relationship.

When you are using multiple indexes, you often want changes to be reflected in several different indexes. dBASE does this automatically anytime that you make a change to a field that is involved in an index. Up to 10 indexes can be open at one time.

The Locate command can search unordered files for relevant records. At the dot prompt when the end of the file is reached, the screen displays the End of LOCATE scope message. If a record is found, locate the next record via the Continue command. When using the Control Center, dBASE automatically goes back to the beginning of the file and starts the search over.

The Seek command can search indexed files for relevant records. You must specify the appropriate index using a Set Order To command (at the dot prompt). If you use the Control Center, the Browse screen displays the records that meet the search criteria.

KEY TERMS AND CONCEPTS

Backward search option
Browse command
concatenate
Continue command
Forward search option
Freeze field option
Index command
Locate command
Match capitalization option
Mixed-data index
multiple-field index

.MDX extension
panning
Record pointer
Seek command
single-field index
Size field option
Skip option
Sort command
String function
updating multiple indexes

CHAPTER QUIZ

Multiple Choice

1. Which of the following statements about sorting is false?
   a. It takes more computer time than indexing.
   b. It takes up more disk space than indexing because an output file has to be created.
   c. A multiple-key sort is simply impossible.
   d. You are allowed to sort on only one field at a time.
   e. All of the above statements are true.

2. Which of the following statements is false about indexing?
   a. The original file is left the same.
   b. The index file that "logically" orders the file is created.
   c. First the index must be accessed and then the data file, if the records are desired in indexed order.
   d. The index holds the contents of each data record.
   e. All of the above statements are true.

3. The _____ command finds records in an unordered file.
   a. Locate
   b. Browse
   c. List
   d. Index
   e. Continue

4. Which of the following commands lets you make changes in a record?
   a. Browse
   b. Locate
   c. Edit
   d. All of the above
   e. None of the above

5. Which command locates records in an indexed file?
   a. Seek
   b. Locate
   c. Skip
   d. Continue
   e. None of the above

True/False

6. You must index a file before using the Locate command.   F

7. The Skip command finds the next record that meets the search criteria   F
   for a sequential search.

8. The indexed field processes an indexed file in sequential order.   T

9. When multiple indexes are specified at the dot prompt, you can use   T
   only the first index name to find records.

10. Sorting files is usually faster than indexing them.   F

Answers

1. c, d   2. d   3. a   4. a, c   5. a   6. f   7. f   8. t   9. t   10. f

Exercises

1. Define or describe each of the following:
   a. index   d. sequential file
   b. multiple-field index   e. indexed file
   c. active index   f. concatenation

2. Use the _Sort_ command to physically reorder the records within a file and create a new file.

3. You can sort the records in a file in either _Asc_ or _Desc_ order.

4. The Sort command sorts files using one or more _Key Fields_

? 5. The _.MDX_ file contains both the key field contents and the record location.

6. Listing records from an indexed file requires dBASE to go to the _index_ file, which then points to the record _number_ in the file.

7. Indexing a file usually takes _less_ time than sorting a file.

8. The process of joining two or more fields to form one index is known as _Concatenation_

? 9. Numeric fields can be included in an index, but they must first be converted to _alpha_ characters.

10. Issue the command _delete_ FILE ZIPCUST to erase the ZIPCUST file.

11. When several indexes follow the Use statement, only the _First_ index can find records.

12. When several indexes are open, a changed field contained in several indexes will result in _Several_ index(es) being updated.

13. The _Seek_ command locates records via an index.

0 14. The _sort_ command locates records in a sequential file.

15. When you are using the Seek command, the character string must appear inside _Quotes_ .

16. The _Skip command_ finds the next record in a sequential file search.

17. The _Browse_ command displays only desired fields when changing or updating records.

Shift+F3 18. The _arrow_ command moves the pointer forward or backward in
" + F4   a field.

19. The _freeze_ option of Browse allows access to only one field.

20. The _F2_ function key switches from Browse to Edit.

. . . .

**COMPUTER
EXERCISES**

The following exercises require the PAYMAST file, created previously.

1. Sort the file by last name. – PrinT

2. Sort the file by gross pay.

3. Index the file by employee ID. List the file.

4. Index the file by last name. List the file.

5. Index the file by gross pay. List the file.

6. Index the file by last name and first name. List the file.

7. Use the last name index to list the file.

8. Find all the employees who have a gross pay of $780.00. Use the Seek command.

9. Use the Locate command to find all the employees that have a pay rate of $4.90.

10. Use the Browse command to examine selected fields of your records.

11. *Student Record Keeping.* You are responsible for maintaining the database for a high school. This database contains information about each student enrolled in school. The student, grades, school data, and information about the student's parents are stored in the file. The database, STUDENTS, has the following structure:

```
STRUCTURE FOR FILE:   A:STUDENTS.DBF
NUMBER OF RECORDS:    00023
DATE OF LAST UPDATE:  11/16/92
PRIMARY USE DATABASE
FLD        NAME       TYPE WIDTH    DEC
001        SFIRST       C    012
002        SMIDDLE      C    001
003        SLAST        C    012
004        SADDRESS     C    025
005        SEX          C    001
006        BIRTHDAY     C    008
007        SSNUMBER     C    011
008        P1FIRST      C    012
009        P1LAST       C    012
010        P1ADDRESS    C    025
011        P1CITY       C    015
012        P1HPHONE     C    013
013        P1OPHONE     C    013
014        P2FIRST      C    012
```

```
015        P2LAST          C      012
016        P2ADDRESS       C      025
017        P2CITY          C      015
018        P2HPHONE        C      013
019        P2OPHONE        C      013
020        DAYSABSENT      N      003
021        SEMGPA          N      004      002
022        OVERALLGPA      N      004      002
023        DISCPTRIPS      N      002
024        HOMEROOM        C      003
025        COUNSELOR       C      020
026        YRINSCHOOL      C      001
027        CLASSES         C      050
** TOTAL **                      00338
```

Let's examine the field contents in each record. The first seven fields contain information about each student: the name, address, sex, birthdate, and Social Security number are stored in these fields.

The NUMBER and the NAME fields can easily be used as index fields to allow easy access to records in the database file. Create the name index by concatenating the SLAST and SFIRST fields to an index called NAME. You will access data by entering the last name followed by the first name.

The fields with a P1 and P2 prefix hold information about the parents. The P1 prefix designates the primary parent, who, especially for children with divorced parents, is the parent with whom the child is living. The P2 prefix entries will, naturally, be the same except for children with divorced or separated parents. Both entries have a HPHONE and OPHONE field to hold a home phone number and office (work) phone number.

The remaining fields hold school-related information for each student. The DAYSABSENT field contains information about the total number of days that a student has missed this school year. This information is critical because state funding is directly related to total days missed for all students in the district.

There are two grade-related fields. The first, SEMGPA, holds information about the current grade-point average (GPA) for a student. The second, OVERALLGPA, contains the student's overall GPA.

The DISCPTRIPS field contains the number of disciplinary trips made to the office by this student. The HOMEROOM field contains the room number for this student's homeroom. The COUNSELOR field contains the name of the counselor assigned to this student. The YRINSCHOOL contains a number that designates the year in school (1 = freshman, 2 = sophomore, 3 = junior, and 4 = senior). The final field, CLASSES, contains the classes (by subject) that are currently being attended by this student.

Your first task is to create the indexes that will be used to access records from the file. Once the indexes have been created and activated for use, add the following student to the database file:

Student Name:	Alan B. Sender
Parents' Name:	John A. Sender
	Marsha L. Sender

Address:	219 Driftwood Ln.
City:	Mobile
Phone:	(412)324-4245
Birthdate:	February 2, 1976
Social Sec. No.:	333-45-7345
Homeroom:	231
Counselor:	
Year:	Sophomore
Classes:	EngIII, U.S. History, PE, Algebra, Spanish II

12. Use the Browse fields command to display each student's first and last name on the screen, as well as the date of birth.

13. LisT oF   Freshmen
               Sophomores
               Juniors   } each on Slast + sFirst
               Seniors   Birthday

               All

DOT PROMPT
COMMANDS,
DELETING RECORDS,
INTRODUCTION TO
REPORTS, AND QUERIES

CHAPTER OBJECTIVES

After completing this chapter, you should be able to:

- **Use a number of commands from the dot prompt**

- **Delete records using both the dot prompt and the Command Center**

- **Use the Report command to generate reports**

- **Create simple and complex queries of a database**

This chapter introduces a number of file manipulation commands using the COMMAND mode and shows how to delete records at the dot prompt and using the Command Center. Finally, it introduces the Report command, which provides control over how a printed report will be generated.

DOT PROMPT COMMANDS

The dBASE package contains a number of useful dot prompt commands that do not have an equivalent command in the Control Center. They include the DIR, List, Display, Replace, and several function and arithmetic commands. In addition, the Delete and Pack commands will be discussed at both the dot prompt and Command Center. You can enter the commands in either lower case or upper case.

To prepare for the exercises in this section, dBASE should be running, and the default drive should be set to drive A (or whichever drive you are using). Invoke the COMMAND mode (dot prompt visible) by pressing Esc and responding Y to the abandon prompt.

DIR

The **DIR command** displays the names of database files already stored on disk. Enter the command below, and a screen like that depicted in Figure 3.1 appears.

```
DIR
```

The DIR command automatically lists only those files containing a .DBF file extension. The DIR command can list other types of files, but to do so requires including the appropriate extension. Enter the command below to list any file containing a .PRG file extension (program files).

```
DIR *.PRG
```

A screen like that depicted in Figure 3.2 now appears.

LIST

The **List command** provides a number of options. For instance, you can exam-ine the file structure, look at all records, specify necessary fields, and specify

Figure 3.1

The output of the DIR command

```
. DIR
Database Files    # Records    Last Update    Size
CUSTOMER.DBF          12        12/23/92      1750
ZIPCUST.DBF           12        12/23/92      1750
ALPHNAME.DBF          12        12/23/92      1750
FIRST.DBF              0        12/23/92        66

    5316 bytes in     4 files
 983552 bytes remaining on drive
.
```

| Command | | | | | NumCaps |

Figure 3.2

The output of the DIR *.PRG command

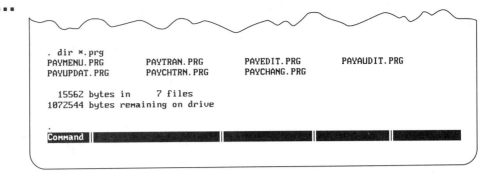

```
. dir *.prg
PAYMENU.PRG        PAYTRAN.PRG        PAYEDIT.PRG        PAYAUDIT.PRG
PAYUPDAT.PRG       PAYCHTRN.PRG       PAYCHANG.PRG

   15562 bytes in      7 files
1072544 bytes remaining on drive
```
Command

Figure 3.3

The output of the List Structure command

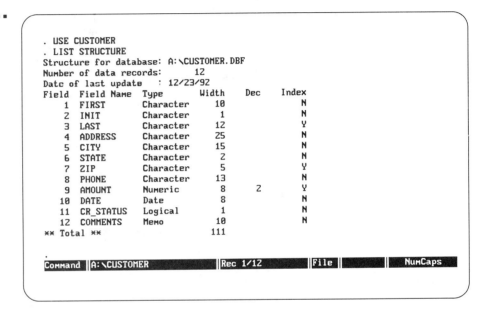

```
. USE CUSTOMER
. LIST STRUCTURE
Structure for database: A:\CUSTOMER.DBF
Number of data records:      12
Date of last update  : 12/23/92
Field  Field Name  Type        Width   Dec   Index
    1  FIRST       Character      10            N
    2  INIT        Character       1            N
    3  LAST        Character      12            Y
    4  ADDRESS     Character      25            N
    5  CITY        Character      15            N
    6  STATE       Character       2            N
    7  ZIP         Character       5            Y
    8  PHONE       Character      13            N
    9  AMOUNT      Numeric         8     2      Y
   10  DATE        Date            8            N
   11  CR_STATUS   Logical         1            N
   12  COMMENTS    Memo           10            N
** Total **                     111
```
Command A:\CUSTOMER   Rec 1/12   File   NumCaps

scope and condition entries to list only the desired records. Before using it, however, invoke the file with the **Use command**.

List Structure   The **List Structure command** lets you examine the structure of a file. Enter the commands below, and a screen like that depicted in Figure 3.3 appears.

```
USE CUSTOMER
LIST STRUCTURE
```

The file structure provides information such as the filename, number of records, date of last update, and the names, data types, and length of all fields. The ** Total ** figure at the bottom of the report is the total number of bytes of storage occupied by each record. Notice that it has a value one greater than the sum of the entries in the Width column. This extra byte of storage allows dBASE to track records that have been marked for deletion. (The Delete command is discussed later.)

The List command is distinct from the List Structure command. It is a **query command** that displays all or selected contents of a file. When the List command is executed, the pointer starts at the top of the file and moves to the bottom. Enter the command below, and a screen like that depicted in Figure 3.4 appears.

```
LIST
```

Figure 3.4

The output of the List command

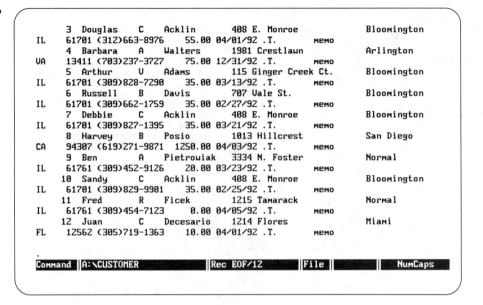

Figure 3.5

The output of the LIST FIRST, INIT, LAST command

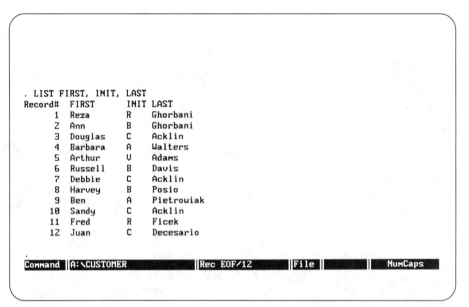

As the command displays the records, they scroll up the screen. Although this line has scrolled off the screen, the field names appear as the first line(s) of the display. When a record is too long to appear on one line, the remaining portion of the record wraps to the next line. The number in the left-most column is the record number. Once the command has executed, the pointer is at the end of the file. This is verified by the `Rec EOF/12` entry in the status line (see Figure 3.4).

List Field   Rather than listing all contents of each record in the file, dBASE can also list only the contents of certain fields by using the field list option. Enter the following command, which lists first names, initials, and last names in the CUSTOMER file:

`LIST FIRST, INIT, LAST`

The records are now listed to the screen (Figure 3.5). Because records are not wrapped to the next line, the listing is more readable than the prior exam-

Figure 3.6

The output of the LIST FIRST, INIT, LAST, AMOUNT command

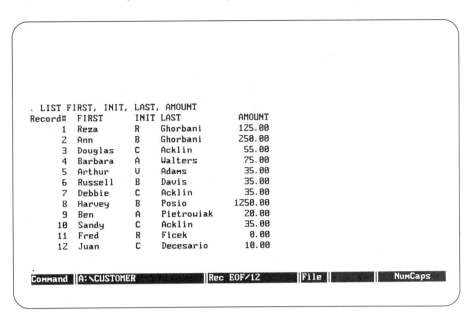

Figure 3.7

The output of the LIST NEXT 5 FIRST, LAST, AMOUNT command

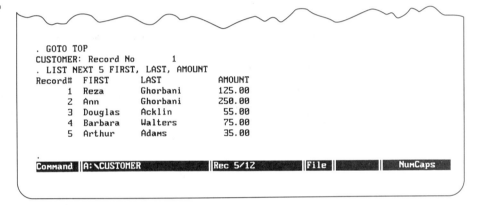

ple and shows the field names that dBASE uses as headings. The `record` number is easier to see in this example.

Try adding the AMOUNT field to the listing you just produced. Enter the command below, and a screen like that depicted in Figure 3.6 appears.

```
LIST FIRST, INIT, LAST, AMOUNT
```

LIST with Scope   You can also use the List command to display the next *x* number of records in a file by adding the **Next option** to the command.

However, because the last List command moved your pointer to the end of the file, first reposition it to the beginning of the file. Enter the commands below, and a screen like that depicted in Figure 3.7 appears.

```
GOTO TOP
LIST NEXT 5 FIRST, LAST, AMOUNT
```

LIST Condition   The List command also displays records that meet a certain criterion by entering the **For parameter** and the selection criterion as part of the List command. For example, the following command lists all records containing an AMOUNT field greater than $100. Enter the command below, and a screen like that depicted in Figure 3.8 appears.

```
LIST FOR AMOUNT > 100
```

Figure 3.8

The output of the LIST FOR AMOUNT > 100 command

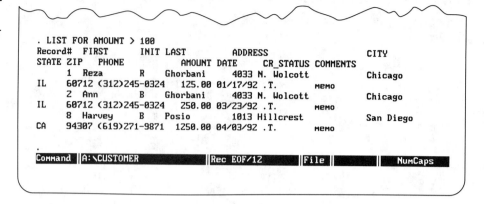

```
. LIST FOR AMOUNT > 100
Record#  FIRST      INIT LAST       ADDRESS                  CITY
STATE ZIP    PHONE          AMOUNT DATE     CR_STATUS COMMENTS
      1  Reza       R    Ghorbani     4033 N. Wolcott       Chicago
IL    60712 (312)245-0324   125.00 01/17/92 .T.      memo
      2  Ann        B    Ghorbani     4033 N. Wolcott       Chicago
IL    60712 (312)245-0324   250.00 03/23/92 .T.      memo
      8  Harvey     B    Posio        1013 Hillcrest        San Diego
CA    94307 (619)271-9871  1250.00 04/03/92 .T.      memo
.
```
```
Command  A:\CUSTOMER              Rec EOF/12      File           NumCaps
```

Figure 3.9

The output of the LIST FIRST, LAST, AMOUNT FOR AMOUNT > 100 command

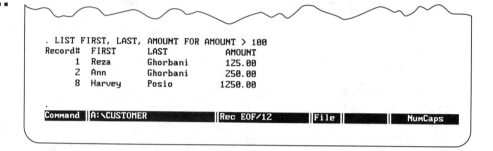

```
. LIST FIRST, LAST, AMOUNT FOR AMOUNT > 100
Record#  FIRST    LAST       AMOUNT
      1  Reza     Ghorbani    125.00
      2  Ann      Ghorbani    250.00
      8  Harvey   Posio      1250.00
.
```
```
Command  A:\CUSTOMER              Rec EOF/12      File           NumCaps
```

Figure 3.10

The output of the Display command

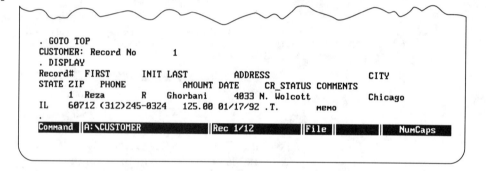

```
. GOTO TOP
CUSTOMER: Record No        1
. DISPLAY
Record#  FIRST      INIT LAST       ADDRESS                  CITY
STATE ZIP    PHONE          AMOUNT DATE     CR_STATUS COMMENTS
      1  Reza       R    Ghorbani     4033 N. Wolcott       Chicago
IL    60712 (312)245-0324   125.00 01/17/92 .T.      memo
.
```
```
Command  A:\CUSTOMER              Rec 1/12        File           NumCaps
```

This command probably generated more output than you need or want. Fortunately, you can tailor the list by combining the field selection and the For criteria within one List command. Enter the command below, and a screen like that depicted in Figure 3.9 appears.

```
LIST FIRST, LAST, AMOUNT FOR AMOUNT > 100
```

DISPLAY

The **Display command**, another form of query, displays the record that is currently at the pointer location. If the pointer is at the bottom of a file (where it would be, for instance, after a List command), the screen does not display a record, but a new dot prompt appears. To view a record with the Display command, first position the pointer to a record. Enter the commands below, and a screen like that depicted in Figure 3.10 appears.

```
GOTO TOP
DISPLAY
```

Figure 3.11

The output of the Display All
command

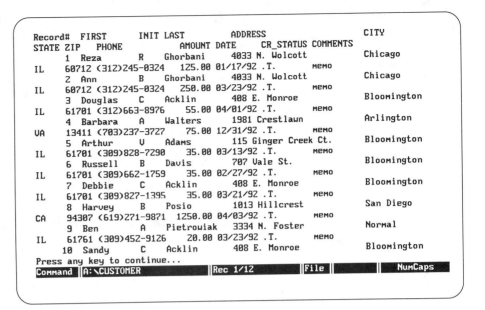

Figure 3.12

The output of the DISPLAY ALL FIRST,
LAST, AMOUNT command

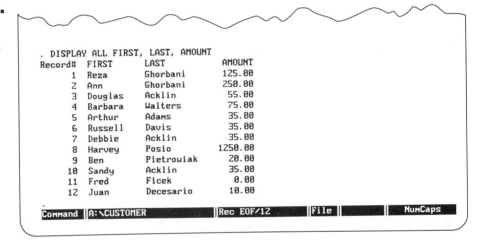

All Scope   The **All scope parameter** of the Display command lists all records
to the screen much as the List command does. The advantage of Display All
is that it displays only 21 lines at a time, rather than scrolling through the
entire file. Enter the command below, and a screen like that depicted in Figure
3.11 appears.

DISPLAY ALL

The Press any key to continue... prompt indicates that another
screen will be displayed when a key is pressed. This will continue until the
end of the file is reached or until Esc is pressed. If the Display command is
interrupted, an *** INTERRUPTED *** message appears at the bottom
of the listing.

The Display All command can use any of the field list, scope, or conditions
options used by the List command. For example, you may want to use this
command to list the FIRST, LAST, and AMOUNT fields. Enter the command
below, and a screen like that depicted in Figure 3.12 appears.

DISPLAY ALL FIRST, LAST, AMOUNT

· ·

Figure 3.13

The output of the LIST FOR CITY = 'Bloomington' command

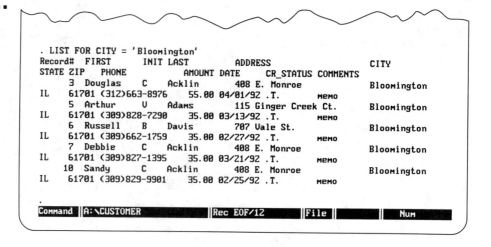

· ·

Figure 3.14

The output of the DISPLAY ALL FIRST, LAST FOR 'Gho' $LAST command

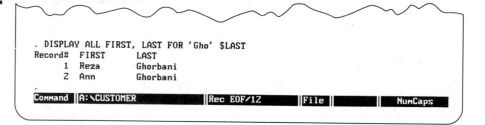

Printing Lists   The List and Display All commands can generate and print crude reports by adding the **To Printer parameter** to the command. For example, the command DISPLAY ALL FIRST, LAST, AMOUNT TO PRINTER generates the printed report. The one disadvantage of this command is that it does not generate column totals or provide more descriptive headings. The Report command, discussed later in this chapter, solves that problem.

Query Using Characters   If you wish to list records based on the contents of a character field, use the List or Display All commands. For example, assume that you wish to list all records that have the CITY field contents of Bloomington. Enter the command below, and a screen like that depicted in Figure 3.13 appears.

```
LIST FOR CITY = 'Bloomington'
```

Query Using Substring Function   Suppose you have a query about a character field, but you don't know the exact contents of the string for which you are searching. You, however, do know several contiguous characters. Such a search requires the use of the **substring function ($)**. For example, to list those records that have the characters *Gho* in the LAST field, enter the command below, and a screen like that depicted in Figure 3.14 appears.

```
DISPLAY ALL FIRST, LAST FOR 'Gho' $LAST
```

The next example lists every record with a capital *A* in the FIRST field. Enter the command below, and a screen like that depicted in Figure 3.15 appears.

```
LIST FIRST, LAST FOR 'A' $FIRST
```

Figure 3.15

The output of the LIST FIRST, LAST FOR 'A' $FIRST command

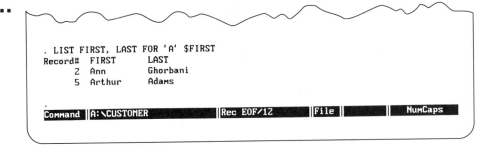

```
. LIST FIRST, LAST FOR 'A' $FIRST
Record#  FIRST      LAST
     2   Ann        Ghorbani
     5   Arthur     Adams

.
Command ||A:\CUSTOMER           ||Rec EOF/12    ||File ||        NumCaps
```

Figure 3.16

The output of the LIST FIRST, LAST FOR 'ar' $FIRST command

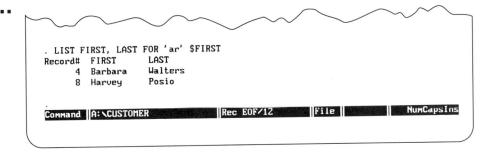

```
. LIST FIRST, LAST FOR 'ar' $FIRST
Record#  FIRST      LAST
     4   Barbara    Walters
     8   Harvey     Posio

Command ||A:\CUSTOMER           ||Rec EOF/12    ||File ||        NumCapsIns
```

The next example lists every record with the characters *ar* in the FIRST field. Enter the command below, and a screen like that depicted in Figure 3.16 appears.

```
LIST FIRST, LAST FOR 'ar' $FIRST
```

dBASE FUNCTIONS

The dBASE package contains some functions that hold instructions for performing a number of tasks that make dBASE easier to use. Several are discussed next.

?   Use the **? character** anytime that you want some piece of information displayed on the screen. It is often used with another command to display the results of a command, function, or the contents of a special dBASE storage area.

Date   If you want to access the system date while you are in dBASE, use the **Date function**. The screen now displays the date that was received by DOS during the boot process; if no date was entered, the screen displays 01/01/80 below the dot prompt. The command and the display are as follows:

```
.? DATE()
```

```
04/01/92
```

The blank between the ? and DATE is optional.

End of File   The **end-of-file (EOF) function** is a way of asking whether you are at the "last" record.

```
.GOTO BOTTOM
.? EOF()
```

Notice that the value returned is F (false), meaning that the end of the file was not detected. This is because the pointer is now at the beginning of the last record. Issue a Skip command to move past the last record:

```
.SKIP
Record no.          13
.? EOF()
```

```
.T.
```

Beginning of File   The same technique applies to the **beginning-of-file (BOF) function**; as shown below, dBASE doesn't realize that it is actually at the top of the file until you try to access a record that isn't there.

```
.GOTO TOP
.?BOF()
```

```
.F.
```

```
.SKIP -1
Record no.           1
.?BOF()
```

```
.T.
```

ARITHMETIC COMMANDS

dBASE has two commands that perform arithmetic using the Sum and Average commands.

Sum   If you want to know the grand total owed in the CUSTOMER file, use the **Sum command**. Enter the command below, and a screen like that depicted in Figure 3.17 appears.

```
SUM AMOUNT
```

You might also be interested in knowing the grand total for customers that have a balance of $100 or more. To determine this, enter the search condition FOR AMOUNT > 100 to the end of the Sum command, and a screen like that depicted in Figure 3.18 appears.

```
SUM AMOUNT FOR AMOUNT > 100
```

Figure 3.17

The output of the SUM AMOUNT command

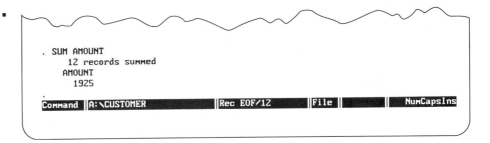

Figure 3.18

The output of the SUM AMOUNT FOR AMOUNT > 100 command

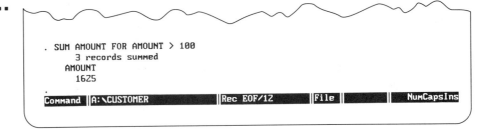

Figure 3.19

The output of the AVERAGE AMOUNT command

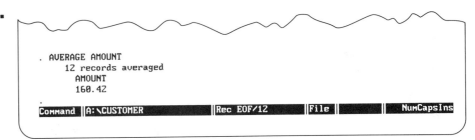

Average   By using the **Average command**, dBASE can also generate the numeric average of a field. For instance, you might want to know the average amount owed in the CUSTOMER file. Enter the command below, and a screen like that depicted in Figure 3.19 appears.

```
AVERAGE AMOUNT
```

REPLACE

You already know how to make changes in a record with the Edit and Browse commands. The **Replace command** also makes changes to a specific record or to all records within a file. Unlike Browse and Edit, however, the Replace command does not display a record before it is changed.

Suppose that Reza Ghorbani paid his bill in full. To change the amount in his record to zero, use the Replace command. Enter the commands below, and a screen like that depicted in Figure 3.20 appears.

```
REPLACE AMOUNT WITH 0 FOR FIRST = 'Reza'
LIST FIRST, LAST, AMOUNT
```

The screen displays the message 1 record replaced. To verify that the Replace command executed correctly, the List command was executed. This example changed only one record. If you want to change every record by the same amount, add the scope parameter All. For example, you could add five cents to each record's amount by issuing a Replace with the All param-

Figure 3.20

The output of the Replace and List commands

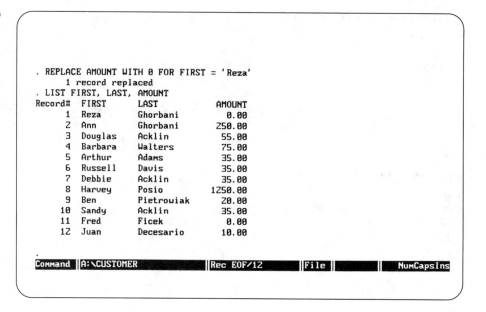

```
.  REPLACE AMOUNT WITH 0 FOR FIRST = 'Reza'
       1 record replaced
.  LIST FIRST, LAST, AMOUNT
Record#   FIRST       LAST          AMOUNT
       1  Reza        Ghorbani        0.00
       2  Ann         Ghorbani      250.00
       3  Douglas     Acklin         55.00
       4  Barbara     Walters        75.00
       5  Arthur      Adams          35.00
       6  Russell     Davis          35.00
       7  Debbie      Acklin         35.00
       8  Harvey      Posio        1250.00
       9  Ben         Pietrowiak     20.00
      10  Sandy       Acklin         35.00
      11  Fred        Ficek           0.00
      12  Juan        Decesario      10.00
.
```

`Command  ║A:\CUSTOMER          ║Rec EOF/12  ║File ║      ║   NumCapsIns`

Figure 3.21

The output of the Replace All and List commands

```
.  REPLACE ALL AMOUNT WITH AMOUNT + .05
      12 records replaced
.  LIST FIRST, LAST, AMOUNT
Record#   FIRST       LAST          AMOUNT
       1  Reza        Ghorbani        0.05
       2  Ann         Ghorbani      250.05
       3  Douglas     Acklin         55.05
       4  Barbara     Walters        75.05
       5  Arthur      Adams          35.05
       6  Russell     Davis          35.05
       7  Debbie      Acklin         35.05
       8  Harvey      Posio        1250.05
       9  Ben         Pietrowiak     20.05
      10  Sandy       Acklin         35.05
      11  Fred        Ficek           0.05
      12  Juan        Decesario      10.05
.
```

`Command  ║A:\CUSTOMER          ║Rec EOF/12  ║File ║      ║   NumCapsIns`

eter. Clearly, if you need to make a change that will affect all records in a file, the Replace All command will do the job faster than the Edit or Browse commands. Enter the commands below, and a screen like that depicted in Figure 3.21 appears.

```
REPLACE ALL AMOUNT WITH AMOUNT + .05
LIST FIRST, LAST, AMOUNT
```

As the Replace command executes, the screen displays the number of each record that is being changed. When the command has finished executing, the screen displays the number of records changed, and the pointer is at the end of the file.

You can easily return the file to its former status by issuing another Replace command. Enter the commands below, and a screen like that depicted in Figure 3.22 appears.

Figure 3.22

The output of the Replace and List commands

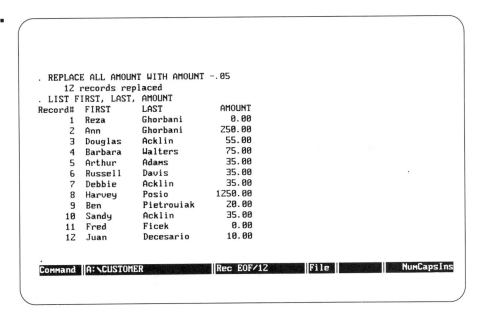

Figure 3.23

The listing to confirm that Reza's record has been changed

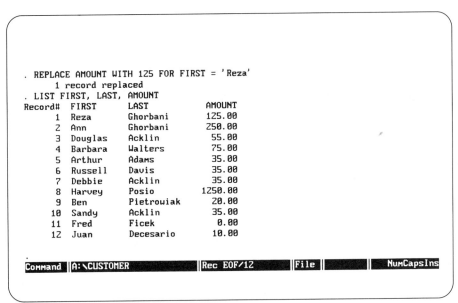

```
REPLACE ALL AMOUNT WITH AMOUNT - .05
LIST FIRST, LAST, AMOUNT
```

Enter the commands below to restore the Reza Ghorbani record back to its prior contents and verify the change. You should see a display like that depicted in Figure 3.23.

```
REPLACE AMOUNT WITH 125 FOR FIRST = 'Reza'
LIST FIRST, LAST, AMOUNT
```

DELETING RECORDS

From time to time, you will want to delete records from a database file. This is a two-step process: (1) The **Delete command** marks the records to be deleted, and (2) the **Pack command** recopies the file with all records that were marked for deletion left out and the rest "packed" together.

Figure 3.24

The record marked for deletion on the Browse screen

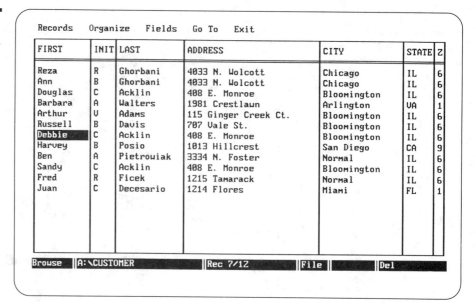

DELETE COMMAND

Marking records for deletion is sometimes referred to as *logical deletion* because, although the record has been marked, it is not yet actually removed from the file and can still be read and processed.

 The following example shows how to mark record 7 for deletion. It assumes that you are in the Control Center. Activate the Browse screen and use the following commands:

↓   Positions to record 7.

F10   Activates the menu bar.

Records   Selects the Records option.

Mark record for deletion   Selects Mark record for deletion.

Enter   Executes the command. A Del message now appears in the status bar (Figure 3.24).

HINTS/HAZARDS   A shortcut for deleting a record entails positioning to the record to be deleted and then entering Ctrl + U from the keyboard.

If you were at the dot prompt and displayed the record, the **delete indicator** (*) would denote that the record had been marked for deletion. If you now move the cursor to another record, the delete entry is recorded to record 7. dBASE places this delete indicator in the first character position of the record. This mark takes up 1 byte of storage on a dBASE record and accounts for the extra position reserved for the fields in a record. The delete indicator makes the marked record easy to spot.

RECALL COMMAND

Until the Pack command is given, the **Recall command** can undelete a record that has been marked for deletion. To undelete a record, first position the

Figure 3.25

dBASE verifies that you wish to recall records

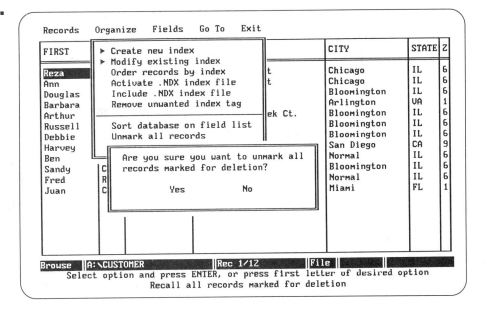

 pointer at that record and then issue the Recall command. The **Recall All command** undeletes any records that have been marked for deletion. Use the following commands to recall record 7:

F10 Activates the menu bar.

Organize Selects the Organize option.

Unmark all records Selects Unmark all records.

Enter Executes the command. An interrogation menu now appears (Figure 3.25).

Type Y Answers Yes. dBASE now displays a message to the screen indicating that one record was recalled.

PACK COMMAND

Once a Pack command is issued, dBASE creates a new copy of the file and copies only those records that have not been marked for deletion to the new file. The old file is erased, and the new file takes its place.

 To practice using the Pack command, add a new record to the end of the file using the following commands. Because this record only illustrates the use of the Pack command, all fields are not filled with data.

↓ Positions the cursor past record 12.

Type Y Answers Yes to the prompt Add new records? (Y/N).

Type Eric Enters the FIRST field contents.

Enter Executes the command.

Type C Enters the INIT field contents.

Type Wild Enters the LAST field contents.

Enter Executes the command.

↑ Records the record to the file.

↓ Positions to record 13.

Ctrl + U   Marks the record for deletion.

F10   Invokes the menu bar.

Organize   Selects the Organize option.

Erase marked records   Selects the Erase marked records option.

Enter   Executes the command.

Type Y   Answers Yes to the dBASE query box.

dBASE now displays a box to the screen, indicating that it is copying the records to the new file. Once this is accomplished, it re-creates each index that is used by the CUSTOMER file. Because six indexes have been created, this command takes a fair amount of time if your default device is a diskette.

INTRODUCTION TO THE REPORT COMMAND

Having data stored in a computerized file is not worth much by itself; for the data to be useful in practical terms, they must be printed in report form. Chapter 1 introduced the Quick Report command. This command, however, did not give you much control over how the information appeared on the report.

Using dBASE's report-generation feature, the **Create Report command**, provides much more flexibility in designing reports. The Create Report command builds a **report template** on disk containing the report format, headings, and fields to be included in the report (see Figure 3.34).

To create the template, respond to various dBASE prompts about the desired characteristics of the report. These are then placed in a file with a .FRM file extension. Whenever you want to print a report using these specifications, activate the report form and use it against the database file that was open when the template was created.

When you use the REPORT feature of dBASE IV, you can create a quick report that is generated automatically by dBASE, or you can design your own report.

QUICK REPORTS

This example illustrates creating a report from scratch. If a file does not have many fields, you can tell dBASE to put the report together and then make changes to the report template. The following example makes use of the database file INVENTRY that resides on your data disk. Either copy that file to the fixed disk or set the default disk to the appropriate diskette drive and invoke that file. Then, from the Control Center, issue the following instructions:

<create>   Selects the <create> option of the Report panel.

Enter   Executes the command. The Report screen to design the report now appears.

Quick layouts   Selects Quick layouts.

Enter   Executes the command.

Column layout   Selects Column layout.

Enter   Executes the command.

↓ (4 times)   Positions to line 3 (see Status bar).

Enter (twice)   Embeds two blank lines in the Page Header Band.

↑, →   Positions the cursor to line 3, column 32.

Figure 3.26

The Report screen for the INVENTRY file

```
 Layout  Fields  Bands  Words  Go To  Print  Exit          4:52:31 PM
[......▼.1...▼....2..▼...3.▼...▼....▼...5..▼..6...▼...7...▼..
 Page     Header  Band─────────────────────────────────────────────────

 Page No. 999
 MM/DD/YY

                              INVENTORY LISTING


 INVID       NAME                              ONHAND  REORDER  OPTIMUM    PRICE

 Report   Intro   Band─────────────────────────────────────────────────
 Detail           Band─────────────────────────────────────────────────
 XXXXXXXXX UUUUUUUUUUUUUUUUUUUUUUUUUUUUUU 999999  9999999  9999999  999999.99
 Report   Summary Band─────────────────────────────────────────────────
                                          999999  9999999  9999999  999999.99
 Page     Footer  Band─────────────────────────────────────────────────


 ──────────────────────────────────────────────────────────────────────
 Report ║A:\<NEW>               ║Line:3 Col:49  ║File:Inventry ║ NumCapsIns
           Add field:F5  Select:F6  Move:F7  Copy:F8  Size:Shift-F7
```

Type INVENTORY LISTING   Enters the title of the report and displays the Report screen like that in Figure 3.26.

You are now ready to test the design to see if it works. Enter the following instructions:

Alt + P   Invokes the Print command in the menu bar.

View report on screen   Selects View report on screen.

Enter   Displays the report to the screen, after a few seconds (Figure 3.27).

Space Bar   Views the rest of the report.

To save the file, issue the following commands:

Alt + E   Invokes the Exit command.

Save changes and exit   Selects Save changes and exit.

Enter   Executes the command.

Type INVLIST   Enters the filename.

Enter   Executes the command.

DESIGNING YOUR OWN REPORT

When you are generating reports, the data presented in a report are typically in some type of order. This means that you are typically using a report template with a sorted or indexed file. To create an entire report in the following example, invoke the CUSTOMER file without using the index. Issue the following commands starting at the Control Center:

<create>   Selects the <create> option of the Reports panel.

Enter   Executes the command.

Esc   Exits the menu box and the Report screen appears (Figure 3.28).

The report specification screen is divided into **bands**, which divide the report into different, logical pieces. These bands can contain fields from the

Figure 3.27

The generated report for the INVENTRY file

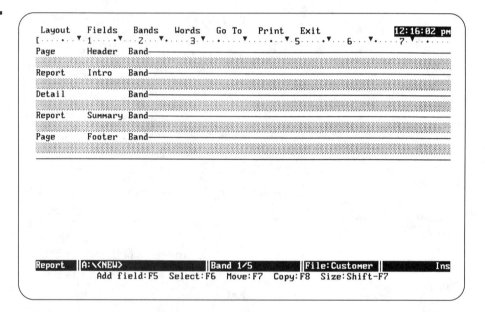

```
Page No.   1
12/24/92
                          INVENTORY LISTING


INVID      NAME                           ONHAND   REORDER  OPTIMUM     PRICE

3625a1     crt lamp                          13       50      100      149.00
4545a1     ready files set                   30       15       45       39.50
8093a1     serial microbuffer               45       30      100      379.00
6137a1     IBM nylon cartridge ribbon       47       35       55        5.95
6582 a1    computer vacuum                  85       75      120      139.00
3970-8a1   multi-purpose back shelf         25       30       50      110.00
4400a1     workstations                      9       12       20      699.00
4430a1     workstations                      5        8       15      650.00
4440       triangle extension               15       18       20      185.00
4442       rectangle extension             100      120      150      175.00
4444       copyholder                       55       50       80       99.00
4446       wristrest                        35       45       50       39.00
4838       footrest                        120      130      150       35.00
4858a1     manager's chair                   8       10       12      549.00
4857       associate's chair                12       15       18      359.00
4856       clerical chair                   33       40       54      299.00
              Cancel viewing: ESC,  Continue viewing: SPACEBAR
```

Figure 3.28

The Report screen used for designing a report

```
 Layout    Fields    Bands    Words    Go To    Print    Exit          12:16:02 pm
[ · · · · · ▼· 1 · · · · ▼· · · ▼· · 3 ▼· · · · · ▼· · · · · · ▼ 5 · · · · ▼· · 6 · · · ▼· · · · 7 · ▼· · · · ·
Page      Header   Band────────────────────────────────────────────────────────

Report    Intro    Band────────────────────────────────────────────────────────

Detail             Band────────────────────────────────────────────────────────

Report    Summary  Band────────────────────────────────────────────────────────

Page      Footer   Band────────────────────────────────────────────────────────




 Report    ║A:\<NEW>                    ║Band 1/5      ║File:Customer ║          Ins
              Add field:F5   Select:F6   Move:F7   Copy:F8   Size:Shift-F7
```

CUSTOMER file, fields created especially for the report, text for titles, or lines and boxes that are drawn for the report. The **Report screen** provides six different **Report Bands**, five of which appear automatically on the screen. The status bar indicates the current band location as well as the file that is being used by dBASE to generate this report. Each band performs the following functions:

- *The Page Header Band* defines the area at the top of each page of the report. It contains information like page numbers, dates, and titles (company name, report name, and column headings).
- The *Report Intro Band* holds data that you want to appear on only the first page. It may contain an explanation of the report.
- *The Detail Band* contains the actual data from the records in the database.

- *The Report Summary Band* contains text and totals that are placed at the end of the report.
- *The Page Footer Band* contains the text or data that are placed at the bottom of each page. Much of the information that is found in the Page Header can also, alternatively, appear in this band.
- *The Group Band* does not automatically appear on the screen. It generates a level break report and subtotals for records that share the same data from one record to the next.

One advantage of using the report generator of dBASE is that the printed report looks just like the template on the screen. This results in more user confidence and no surprises when the report is finally printed. Your cursor should be in the Page Header Band.

1. The following commands place the date in the Page Header Band:

   Alt + F   Invokes the Fields option of the menu bar.

   Add field   Selects `Add field`.

   Enter   Displays a picklist menu of all possible fields that can be included in the report (Figure 3.29).

   Date   Selects the `Date` option in the PREDEFINED column.

   Enter   Displays a screen (Figure 3.30) that lets you determine how the data will be displayed (pictured) on the report.

   Ctrl + End   Places the date in the Page Header Band.

2. The following instructions place the page number in the Page Header Band:

   ↓   Positions the cursor to line 0 (see status bar).

   Enter   Inserts a blank line in the Page Header Band.

   Alt + F   Invokes the Fields option of the menu bar.

   Enter   Executes the `Add field` command.

   Pageno   Selects the `Pageno` option in the PREDEFINED column.

   Enter   Executes the command.

   Template   Selects `Template` of the Template menu.

   Enter   Executes the command.

   Home   Goes to the beginning of the field.

   Ins   Toggles INSERT mode on, if the Ins indicator does not appear in the status bar.

   Type Page   Enters the word *Page* followed by a space.

   Enter   Executes the command.

   Ctrl + End   Places the field in the report.

3. Now specify which fields to print and then go back and specify the heading information. In creating the Detail Band, use the FIRST, LAST, ADDRESS, CITY, STATE, and AMOUNT fields:

   ↓ **(4 times)**   Positions to line 0 of the Detail Band.

   ← **(4 times)**   Positions to column 4 of the Detail Band. Unless

Figure 3.29

The Report picklist menu

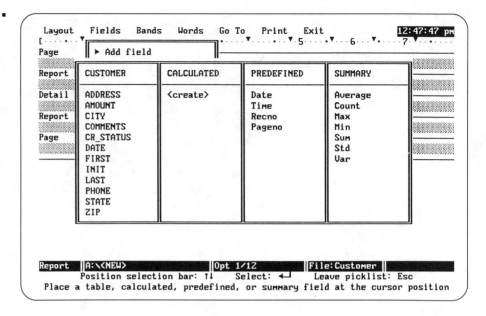

Figure 3.30

The menu box for determining the
display attributes of a field

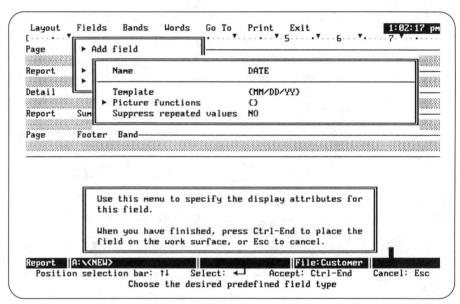

this command is issued, dBASE automatically leaves an eight-
position left-hand margin.

4. Add the data fields to the report:

> **Alt + F** Invokes the Fields option of the menu bar.
>
> **Enter** Invokes the Add Field command.
>
> **FIRST** Selects the FIRST field in the CUSTOMER column.
> Notice that the fields appear in alphabetic order.
>
> **Enter** Executes the command.
>
> **Ctrl + End** Inserts the field in the report.

Figure 3.31

The definition screen shows each field as it is added

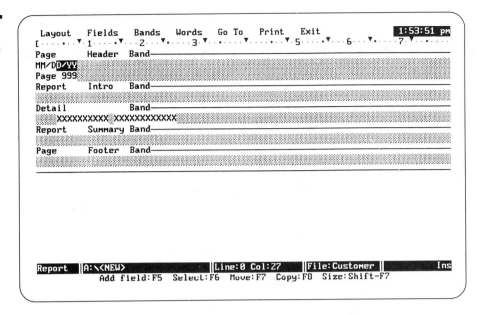

→   Moves the cursor to the right one position. This leaves room for the next field to be added to the template. If you forget to insert a space before you add the next field, press Backspace to erase the field and then insert the space. The new field can then be added to the report.

Alt + F   Invokes the Fields option of the menu bar.

Enter   Invokes the Add Field command.

LAST   Selects the LAST field in the CUSTOMER column.

Enter   Executes the command.

Ctrl + End   Inserts the field in the report.

→   Moves the cursor to the right one position.

Notice that as fields are added to the Detail Band, the template reflects the changes (Figure 3.31).

5. Add the rest of the data fields:

Alt + F   Invokes the Fields option of the menu bar.

Enter   Invokes the Add Field command.

ADDRESS   Selects the ADDRESS field in the CUSTOMER column.

Enter   Executes the command.

Ctrl + End   Inserts the field in the report.

6. Resize the ADDRESS field so that it takes up less space on the line, using the following commands:

Left Arrow   Selects the ADDRESS field.

Shift + F7   Issues the Resize command.

← (5 times)   Moves the cursor five spaces to the left.

Enter   Executes the command.

→ (twice)   Moves the cursor to the right two spaces, to make room for the next field.

Alt + F   Invokes the Fields option of the menu bar.

Enter   Invokes the `Add Field` command.

CITY   Selects the `CITY` field in the CUSTOMER column.

Enter   Executes the command.

Ctrl + End   Inserts the field in the report.

→   Moves the cursor to the right one position.

Alt + F   Invokes the Fields option of the menu bar.

Enter   Invokes the `Add Field` command.

STATE   Selects the `STATE` field in the CUSTOMER column.

Enter   Executes the command.

Ctrl + End   Inserts the field in the report.

→   Moves the cursor to the right one position.

Alt + F   Invokes the Fields option of the menu bar.

Enter   Invokes the `Add Field` command.

AMOUNT   Selects the `AMOUNT` field in the CUSTOMER column.

Enter   Executes the command.

Ctrl + End   Inserts the field in the report.

→   Moves the cursor to the right one position.

You have now finished with the Detail Band and should have a screen like that depicted in Figure 3.32.

7. The following commands place the headings in the Page Header Band. This information is the company name, report name, and column headings:

↑ (4 times)   Positions the cursor to the Page Header Band.

Enter   Inserts a line in the header.

→   Positions to line 2, column 35.

Type ABC COMPANY   Enters the name of the company.

Enter   Inserts a blank line.

→   Positions to line 3, column 24.

Type CUSTOMER NAME AND ADDRESS REPORT   Enters the name of the report.

Enter (twice)   Inserts a blank line.

→   Positions to line 5, column 15.

Type NAME   Enters the column heading.

→   Positions to line 5, column 28.

Type ADDRESS   Enters the column heading.

→   Positions to line 5, column 49.

Type CITY   Enters the column heading.

→   Positions to line 5, column 65.

Type ST.   Enters the column heading.

Figure 3.32

The completed Detail Band

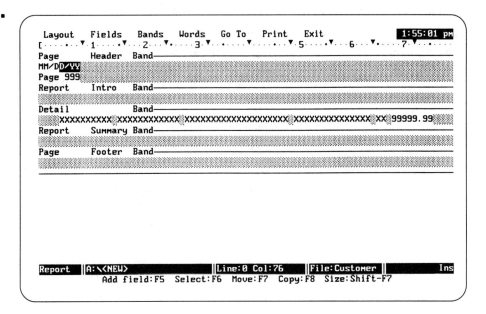

→   Positions to line 5, column 69.

Type AMOUNT   Enters the column heading.

8. You are now ready to specify the total for the AMOUNT field in the Report Summary Band:

   ↓   Positions to line 0 of the Report Summary Band.

   →   Positions to line 0, column 66 (underneath and slightly to the left of the AMOUNT field).

   Alt + F   Invokes the fields option of the menu bar.

   Enter   Invokes the Add field command.

   Sum   Selects the Sum entry of the SUMMARY column.

   Enter   Executes the command.

   Field to summarize on   Selects Field to summarize on.

   Enter   Opens the Field specification submenu.

   AMOUNT   Selects the AMOUNT field.

   Enter   Executes the command.

   Ctrl + End   Inserts the field.

Your Report screen should now look like that depicted in Figure 3.33.

9. You are now ready to test the report template by using the following commands:

   Alt + P   Invokes the Print command from the menu bar.

   View report on screen   Selects the View report on screen option.

   Enter   Executes the command.

Several seconds elapse while dBASE assembles the various parts of the template; then dBASE creates and compiles the various programs. After

Figure 3.33

The completed report template

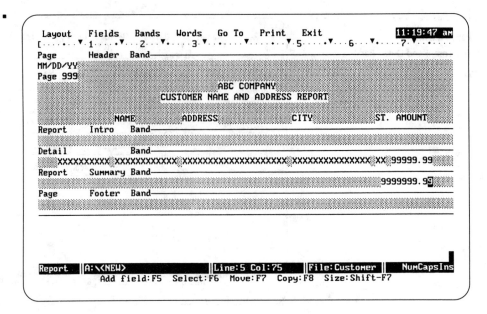

Figure 3.34

The report viewed on the screen

a few seconds, a screen like that depicted in Figure 3.34 appears on the monitor.

10. You are now ready to save the template to disk. To do this, use the following commands:

> **Alt + E**   Invokes the Exit menu from the menu bar.
>
> **Save changes and exit**   Selects Save changes and exit.
>
> **Enter**   Executes the command.
>
> **Type NAMEADDR**   Enters the name of the file to be saved.

USING THE REPORT FILE FROM THE CONTROL CENTER

The report file NAMEADDR just created can be used with only the CUSTOMER file. Once the CUSTOMER file has been invoked, issue the following commands from the Control Center:

NAMEADDR   Selects the NAMEADDR file in the Report panel.

Enter   Executes the command.

Print report   Selects the Print report option.

Enter   Executes the command.

Begin printing   Selects the Begin printing option.

Enter   Executes the command.

USING THE REPORT FORM FROM THE DOT PROMPT

Once the template has been saved to disk, you can invoke it from the dot prompt using the **Report Form command** REPORT FORM NAMEADDR. If you forgot the USE CUSTOMER command, dBASE prompts you for the filename. The report is then displayed to the screen. The following command sends the output to the printer: REPORT FORM NAMEADDR TO PRINTER.

You can also use selection criteria for including records in a report at the dot prompt. For example, if you want to only include records with the CITY field contents of Bloomington, use the following command.

REPORT FORM NAMEADDR FOR CITY = 'Bloomington' TO PRINTER

To receive a report containing all customers with a balance over $35.00, use this command:

REPORT FORM NAMEADDR FOR AMOUNT > 35.00 TO PRINTER

We introduced entering elementary queries at the dot prompt, using the List and Display commands. This section introduces you to the Query command that is activated from the Queries panel of the Control Center.

Recall that a simple query at the dot prompt contains a query command, one field to be examined, a relational operator, and some value:

```
LIST FOR CITY = 'Normal'
```

In this example, only those records containing the value *Normal* in the CITY field will be displayed. The **relational operator** is the equal sign (=). Other relational operators that can appear in a query are the following:

<	Less than
>	Greater than
=	Equal to
<> or #	Not equal
<=	Less than or equal
>=	Greater than or equal
$	Substring comparison (for example, if fields NAME1 and NAME2 contain character data, NAME1$NAME2 returns a logical True if NAME1 is either identical to NAME2 or contained within NAME2)

When the query requires examining several fields, the selection criteria for the fields must be linked with the following **logical operators** (note that periods are required before and after):

.NOT.	The opposite of this expression must occur for this action to take place.
.AND.	This condition requires that both conditions be true before any action will be taken.
.OR.	This condition requires that only one of the conditions be true for the action to be taken.
( )	Parentheses group relations together. If nested parentheses are used, dBASE evaluates an expression by starting with the innermost set and working outward.

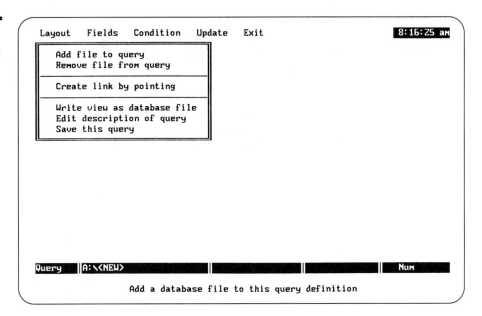

FILE USED BY QUERY

When you use the Queries option of the Control panel to create a view query,
dBASE places the conditions that you specify in a .QBE file. Once the view
query has been defined and saved, you can recall it, using the Queries panel,
to locate records that meet the specified conditions.

CREATING A QUERY SPECIFICATION

The Queries panel of the Control Center lets you create a view query using
the Query screen. Once the <create> command is executed, the screen displays a menu like that depicted in Figure 3.35.

> **<create>** Selects the ⟨ c r e a t e ⟩ option of the Queries panel.
>
> **Enter** Executes the command.
>
> **A** Selects the Add file to query option of the Layout
> submenu.
>
> **CUSTOMER.DBF** If no file is invoked, a picklist containing the files
> is displayed to the screen (Figure 3.36). Highlight the CUSTOMER file.
> If you accidentally highlight the wrong file, issue the Layout (Alt + L)
> command and then select the Remove file from query command.
>
> **Enter** The screen displays the file skeleton (Figure 3.37).

The file skeleton Customer.dbf entry contains the filename, and the fields
are in order to the right of that entry. The field width of the display is deter-
mined by the size of the field name, not the number of characters contained
in the field. You can move to the right via the Tab command and to the left

Figure 3.36

The picklist of files

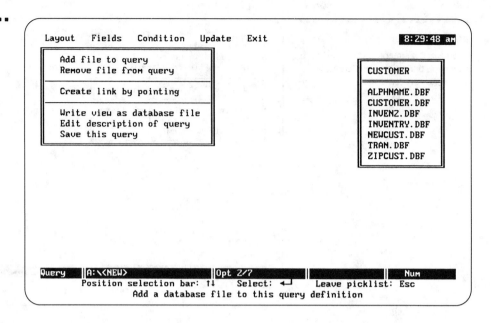

Figure 3.37

The file skeleton of the CUSTOMER file

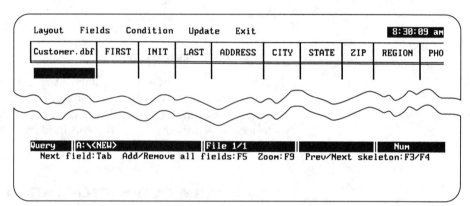

using Shift + Tab. As you move beyond the last field, the field bar moves back to the beginning of the display. Once you position the cursor to a field that extends beyond the original screen width, an arrow appears on the line beneath the Customer.dbf box indicating the direction in which the beginning of the skeleton lies.

The F3 and F4 function keys determine in which skeleton the cursor will appear. F3 moves the cursor up to the next skeleton, and F4 moves the cursor down to the next skeleton.

Adding Fields to the Query   Once your file skeleton is present, you can include a field by positioning the cursor to that field and selecting the Add field entry from the Fields submenu. You can also use a shortcut by highlighting the field and then pressing F5:

1. The following commands add the FIRST, LAST, and AMOUNT fields to the View Query specification at the bottom of the screen:

> **Tab**   Positions the cursor to the FIRST field.
>
> **Alt + F**   Invokes the Fields submenu.

Figure 3.38

The completed View Query specification

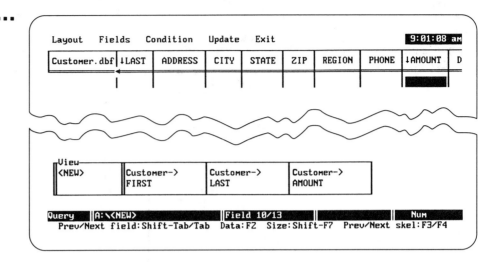

A   Selects the Add field to view command. A Down Arrow now appears in the FIRST field of the skeleton to indicate that the field has been selected and the field is placed in the View skeleton at the bottom of the screen.

Tab (twice)   Positions the cursor to the LAST field.

F5   Selects the Add field to view command.

Tab (7 times)   Positions the cursor to the AMOUNT field.

F5   Selects the Add field to view command. You should now have a View Query specification screen like that depicted in Figure 3.38. The entries at the bottom of the screen compose the View skeleton that controls which fields are displayed.

2. Once you have completed the View Query specification, test the View query by issuing the following commands:

F2   Selects the Data command to display a Browse screen like that depicted in Figure 3.39. This lets you see if the query is executing properly.

Shift + F2   Issues the Design command to return to the View Query specification screen.

3. Save the View Query file to disk:

Alt + E   Invokes the Exit submenu of the menu bar.

S   Selects the Save changes and exit command.

Type LFAMOUNT   Enters the filename.

Enter   Saves the file to disk (after several seconds of processing) and returns you to the Control Center.

4. To use the View Query file later, issue the following instructions:

LFAMOUNT   Selects the LFAMOUNT entry of the Queries panel.

....

Figure 3.39

The Browse screen created via the View Query specification

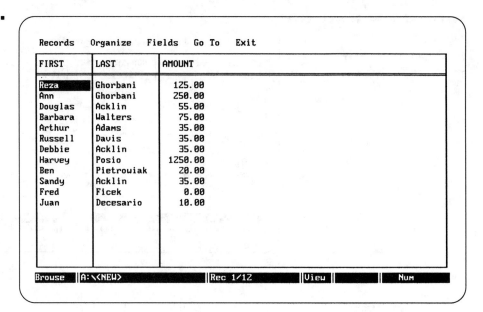

FIRST	LAST	AMOUNT
Reza	Ghorbani	125.00
Ann	Ghorbani	250.00
Douglas	Acklin	55.00
Barbara	Walters	75.00
Arthur	Adams	35.00
Russell	Davis	35.00
Debbie	Acklin	35.00
Harvey	Posio	1250.00
Ben	Pietrowiak	20.00
Sandy	Acklin	35.00
Fred	Ficek	0.00
Juan	Decesario	10.00

Browse   A:\<NEW>   Rec 1/12   View   Num

Enter Executes the command.

D Selects the Display data command. A Browse screen like that depicted in Figure 3.39 appears on your monitor.

The LFAMOUNT and View entries in the status bar indicate the name of the View Query file in use.

SPECIFYING A CONDITION

You may wish to specify specific **conditions** that are to be used for including records for a specific application. The following example uses a relational operator to locate all records with a 61701 ZIP code:

LFAMOUNT Selects the LFAMOUNT entry in the Queries panel.

Enter Executes the command.

M Selects the Modify query command.

Alt + C Invokes the Condition submenu from the menu bar.

A Selects the Add condition box command and displays a condition box on the screen.

Type ZIP = '61701' Enters the condition.

Enter Executes the command. The condition box should look like that depicted in Figure 3.40.

F2 Displays the records that meet this criterion on the Browse screen (Figure 3.41).

Shift + F2 Returns you to the Query screen.

Once you have performed the query using the condition, the condition can be disabled by selecting the Delete condition box option of the

Figure 3.40

The completed condition box

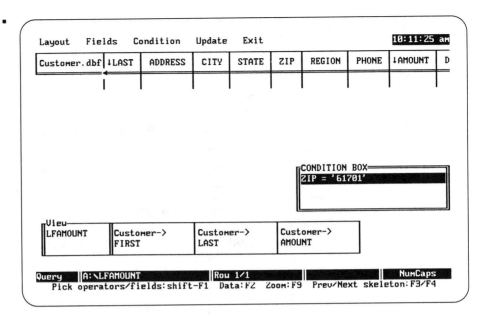

Figure 3.41

The records accessed via the View Query condition

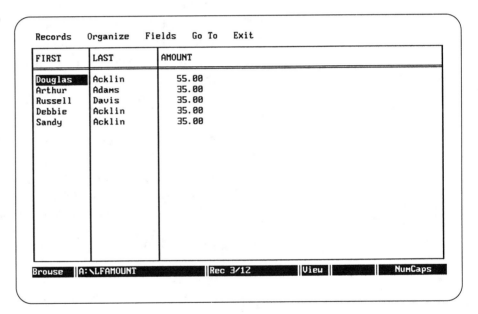

Condition menu. If you again use the Data (F2) command, all records are again available.

HINTS/HAZARDS	If you want to get out of a condition box without entering a condition, invoke the Condition menu (Alt + C) and execute the Delete condition box command.

SPECIFYING MULTIPLE CONDITIONS

Assume that you want to list any records in the CUSTOMER file from Chicago or San Diego that contain an amount owed greater than $100. This query requires both logical and relational operators and is specified in a condition box as CITY = 'Chicago' .AND. AMOUNT > 100 .OR. CITY = 'San Diego' .AND. AMOUNT > 100. It is to include the following fields: FIRST, LAST, ADDRESS, CITY, STATE, and AMOUNT.

1. To start, use the following commands:

    <create>   Selects the ⟨create⟩ option of the Queries panel.

    Enter   Executes the command.

    A   Selects the Add file to query command.

    CUSTOMER   Selects CUSTOMER from the picklist.

    Enter   Executes the command.

2. Add the fields using the following commands:

    Tab to FIRST, F5   Goes to and adds the FIRST field to the file.

    Tab to LAST, F5   Goes to and adds the LAST field to the file.

    Tab to ADDRESS, F5   Goes to and adds the ADDRESS field to the file.

    Tab to CITY, F5   Goes to and adds the CITY field to the file.

    Tab to STATE, F5   Goes to and adds the STATE field to the file.

    Tab to AMOUNT, F5   Goes to and adds the AMOUNT field to the file.

3. Enter the condition:

    Alt + C   Invokes the Condition submenu.

    A   Selects Add condition box command.

    Type CITY = 'Chicago' .AND. AMOUNT > 100 .OR. CITY = 'San Diego' .AND. AMOUNT > 100   Enters the condition. After the condition has been entered, the condition box is not large enough to display all of the text.

    F9   Issues the Zoom command to expand the condition box. Your screen should now look like that in Figure 3.42.

    F2   Issues the Data command to display the Browse screen (Figure 3.43). If you have an error in the condition, an error message appears on the screen. Press F9 (Zoom command) to expand the box and edit the condition entry. Ensure that periods precede and follow the logical operators and that the fields have been spelled properly.

    Shift + F2   Returns you to the Query screen.

    If you are building a condition and forget the name of a field or how to specify a relational or logical condition, issue the Pick operators/fields (Shift + F1) command to invoke the menu like that depicted in Figure 3.44. Highlight the desired entry and press Enter to tell dBASE to automatically include that entry in the condition box.

4. Save the query using the name GT100:

    Alt + E   Invokes the Exit menu.

    S   Selects the Save changes and exit command. You can

Figure 3.42

The condition as viewed using the Zoom (F9) command

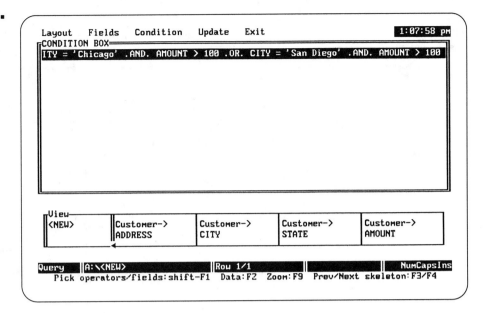

Figure 3.43

The records displayed to Browse using multiple conditions

also issue the Layout (Alt + E) command and then execute the `Save this query` command.

Type GT100   Enters the filename.

Using a Query with Other dBASE Commands   Once the query file has been created, use it to update or print just those records specified. To do this, first activate the appropriate query file and then issue another dBASE command from the Control Center. The following example generates a report using the GT100 View Query file:

GT100   Selects the `GT100` entry of the Queries panel.

Enter   Executes the command.

Figure 3.44

The Pick operators/fields menu

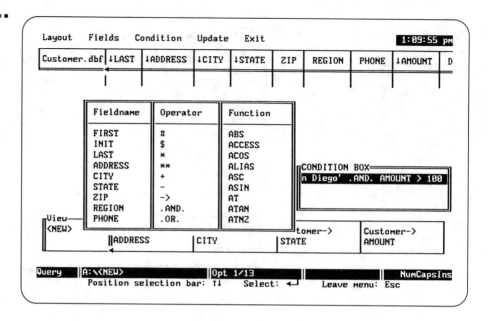

Figure 3.45

The report generated via the
NAMEADDR report template using
the GT100 query file

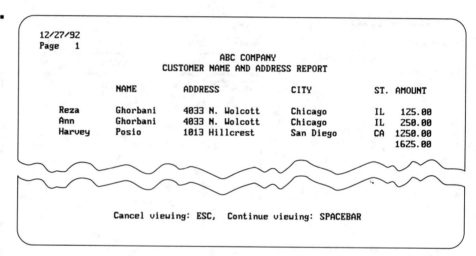

U Selects the Use view command.

NAMEADDR Selects the NAMEADDR entry of the Reports panel.

Enter Executes the command.

P Selects the Print report command.

C Selects the Current view command.

V Selects the View report on screen command. The screen
displays a report containing only those records that meet the selection
criteria (Figure 3.45).

HINTS/HAZARDS

When you use query files to control other dBASE commands, make certain that the fields included in the Query specifications match those contained in the other dBASE application to be executed. Otherwise, errors may result in undesirable output.

THE QUERY AT THE DOT PROMPT

To create a query file from the dot prompt requires using the **Create Query** command. To build the query file, issue the following command:

```
CREATE QUERY LFAMOUNT
```

Figure 3.46

The output of the SUM operator

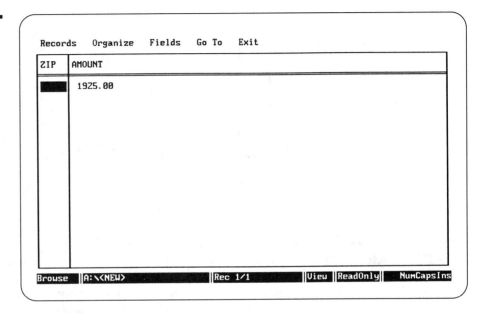

Figure 3.47

The Query entries for obtaining the average for each ZIP code

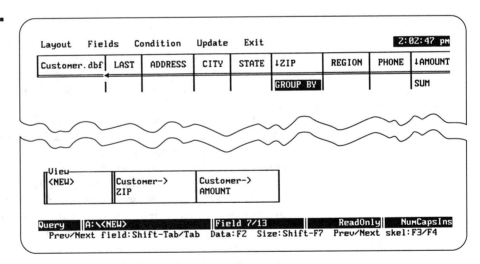

Figure 3.48

The output of the Group by ZIP for AMOUNT

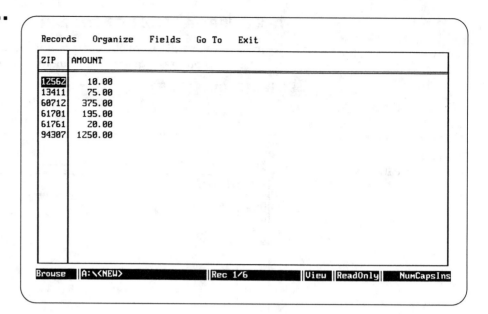

```
      Records   Organize   Fields   Go To   Exit
   ┌──────┬───────────────────────────────────────────────────────┐
   │ ZIP  │ AMOUNT                                                  │
   ├──────┼                                                         │
   │ 12562│   10.00                                                 │
   │ 13411│   75.00                                                 │
   │ 60712│  375.00                                                 │
   │ 61701│  195.00                                                 │
   │ 61761│   20.00                                                 │
   │ 94307│ 1250.00                                                 │
   │      │                                                         │
   │      │                                                         │
   │      │                                                         │
   └──────┴───────────────────────────────────────────────────────┘
   Browse   ║A:\<NEW>              ║Rec 1/6        ║View ║ReadOnly║  NumCapsIns
```

CHAPTER REVIEW

The dBASE package provides commands for manipulating data. The List command displays (a) the contents of an entire file, (b) selected records, (c) selected fields of records, or (d) the file structure. The Display All command works like the List command but stops when it has displayed 21 lines.

The Replace command changes one record, selected groups of records, or all records in the field at one time, in accordance with selection criteria. This command provides another method, besides the Edit and Browse commands, for changing the field contents of records.

The substring function ($) is a powerful command that searches for characters in a field of data. It can be used with commands such as Replace and List.

The dBASE package does not automatically delete a record from a file when you issue the Delete command. Instead, it marks the record with dBASE's delete indicator, the asterisk (*), for future deletion. After a record has been marked for deletion, it can be undeleted with the Recall command. Physically removing a record from a file requires the Pack command following the Delete command. The Pack command copies the entire file to a new location on disk, dropping any records marked for deletion, and deletes the previous file.

The Create Report command lets you format a report via a report template for information contained in a file. The Create Report feature provides a number of bands for you to use in describing the report, including bands for specifying report and column headings and any fields you want to print. A band also generates totals for any numeric fields.

The dBASE IV package lets you create simple and complex queries at the dot prompt or build them using the Control Center. Because many keystrokes are required, frequently used queries should be saved to a .QBE file.

KEY TERMS AND CONCEPTS

All scope parameter
Average command bands
beginning-of-file (BOF) function
condition
Create Query command
Create Report command
Date function
Delete command
delete indicator (*)
DIR command
Display command
end-of-file (EOF) function
For parameter
List command
List Structure command
logical operator
Next option

Pack command
QBE extension
QBO extension
query command
query file
Recall All command
Recall command
relational operator
Replace command
Report Band
Report Form command
Report screen
report template
substring function ($)
Sum command
To Printer parameter
Use command
? character

CHAPTER QUIZ

Multiple Choice

1. Which of the following dBASE commands change records in a file?
   a. List
   b. Edit
   c. Report
   d. Replace
   e. Change

2. If you use the To Printer parameter, reports could be generated using which of the following statements?
   a. List
   b. Report
   c. Display
   d. All of the above

3. The Report feature of dBASE lets you do which of the following?
   a. Establish a report title
   b. Print column headings
   c. Number each page
   d. Print totals
   e. All of the above
   f. Only a, b, and c

4. Which of the following Report Bands is used to hold page numbers?
   a. Page Header
   b. Report Intro
   c. Detail Band
   d. Report Summary
   e. Page Footer

5. Which of the following statements is true about the List and Display commands?
   a. Display does not display selected fields.
   b. Both List and Display prohibit arithmetic selection criteria.
   c. Display All shows the next 21 lines and then pauses.
   d. Display automatically lists all records in the file.
   e. All of the above statements are true.

True/False

6. The Display All command gives you more control than the simple List command.

7. The Delete command physically removes a record from a file.

8. The Recall command automatically unerases all deleted records within a file.

9. The Display command shows the record at the current pointer location.

10. The Sum command can be used to total numeric fields from selected records.

Answers

1. b, d   2. d   3. e   4. a   5. c   6. t   7. f   8. f   9. t   10. t

Exercises

1. The command Display _____ displays all records in the file on the screen and pauses after every 21 lines.

2. The _____ command displays the record at the current pointer location.

3. List three pointer positioning commands.

4. The _____ command changes records in the file.

5. The function _____ finds a character string in a field.

6. The _____ command marks a record for deletion.

7. The _____ command undeletes a record.

8. The _____ command removes records from a file that have been marked for deletion.

9. The _____ command generates the total of a field from the records in a file.

10. The _____ command parameter sends any output on the screen to the printer.

11. The _____ command of the Report panel builds a report template that can be used later.

12. The _____ Band contains the data field in a report template.

13. The report template assumes that the _____ file is to be used if a Print command is given for a report template.

14. The _____ Band of the Report screen generates totals of numeric columns.

15. The _____ option generates reports quickly.

16. A complex query typically makes use of one or more relational operators as well as one or more _____ operators.

17. The _____ command groups records in a query.

18. The _____ at the dot prompt (.) invokes a query file.

19. The logical operators are _____, _____, and _____.

20. A query file created by dBASE contains a _____ file extension.

The following exercises require using the PAYMAST file, created previously.

1. Look at the format of the database records.

2. Look at the employee and pay rate of each record.

3. Look at only those employees with a gross of more than $850.

4. Total the GROSS PAY field.

5. Total the GROSS PAY field for those with a gross of more than $900.

6. Give Mark Tell a raise of .50.

7. Give everyone a raise of .25.

8. Go to record 5 and display it to the screen.

9. Delete and recall record 9.

10. Delete record 5.

11. Pack the file.

12. Use the $ function to find any record with a *P* in the first or last name.

13. Create the following report and print it.

```
PAGE NO. 00001
04/13/92


                                        PAYROLL SUMMARY


        I.D.      EMPLOYEE                PAY RATE          GROSS
        4908  Richard    Payne             4.45           556.00
        5789  Connie     Reiners           3.35           450.00
        5523  Pamela     Rich              6.00           780.00
        6324  Mark       Tell              5.50           980.00
        2870  Frank      Terlep            6.80           670.00
        4679  Kenneth    Klass             4.90           780.00
        8345  Thomas     Momery            4.70           580.00
        5649  Toni       McCarthy          5.20           667.00
        5432  Alan       Monroe            5.20          1340.00
        5998  Paul       Mish              4.90           887.00
        4463  Edward     Mockford          4.90           775.00
         456                               0.00             0.00
        ** TOTAL **

                                                         8465.00
```

14. Use the report template you developed to generate a report for employees with a gross pay of more than $800.

15. Indicate which parts of the following commands correspond with the command, scope, noun, and condition portions of a dBASE command. For example, in the command LIST NEXT 5 FIRST, LAST, ADDRESS

FOR AMOUNT > 50: the command is LIST; the scope is NEXT 5; the nouns are FIRST, LAST, and ADDRESS; and the condition is FOR AMOUNT > 50.

```
a.   DIR
b.   DIR *.DBF
c.   LIST FIRST, LAST, CITY, STATE
d.   USE ACCREC
e.   DELETE ALL
f.   REPLACE NAME WITH ADOLPH FOR LAST = 'HITLER'
g.   REPORT FORM NAMEADDR FOR AMOUNT > 100
h.   CREATE REPORT
i.   DISPLAY ALL FIRST,LAST
j.   REPLACE AMOUNT WITH 0 FOR STATE = 'Il'
k.   SUM AMOUNT FOR AMOUNT > 50
l.   LIST NEXT 7
```

16. Use the PAYMAST file with the last name index and print the report.

17. Use the PAYMAST file with the gross pay index and print the report.

18. This exercise requires the STUDENT file. For information about the structure of this file, refer to the exercises in Chapter 2.

    Create a report template, STUDQRY, that corresponds to the following format:

```
PAGE NO.     1
04/21/92


                    Some School Name
               Student Query Listing
Name                Address                  Homeroom
Jane     Abbott     1800 W. Barker Ave       133
Duane    Ackerman   2893 Malone St.          346
```

    a. Run this report from the Control Center to include all records from the file.
    b. From the dot prompt, issue the command that will include only those students who have an overall GPA of over 3.5.
    c. From the dot prompt, issue the command that will include only those students who have three or more disciplinary visits to the office.
    d. The next task involves answering a number of questions using commands from the dot prompt.

       ■ Find how many female students are in all grades.
       ■ Find the total days missed by students.
       ■ Calculate the average number of days missed per student.
       ■ Calculate the average GPA of the students.
       ■ Find how many students are in each grade.

19. Use a query file to set up the following query for the CUSTOMER file:
    ZIP = 61761 and AMOUNT > 50 .OR. CITY = BLOOMINGTON.

dBASE IV 1.1
COMMAND
SUMMARY

CONVENTIONS

Lower case	User-supplied information
Upper case	Explicit portions of dBASE IV 1.1 commands
[. . .]	Optional portions of dBASE IV 1.1 commands
<. . .>	User-supplied portions of dBASE IV 1.1 commands
<cstring>	Character strings
<exp>	Valid item or group of items and/or operators
<exp list>	List of expressions separated by commas
<field>	Record field name
<field list>	List of record field names separated by commas
<file>	Name of a file to access or create
<index file>	Name of an index file to create or access
<key>	Portion(s) of a file used to create an index file
<n>	Number that dBASE IV 1.1 is to regard as a literal value
<numeric exp>	An <exp> whose content is defined as numeric
<scope>	Command option that specifies a range of records that dBASE IV 1.1 must treat in executing a command; has three possible values: ALL records in the file; NEXT *n* records in the file; and RECORD *n* (default value varies from command to command)
<skeleton>	Allows batch manipulation of files of the same type and/or having matching strings in filename

OPERATORS

LOGICAL OPERATORS (IN ORDER OF PRECEDENCE)

( )	Parentheses for grouping
.NOT.	Logical not
.AND.	Logical and
.OR.	Logical or
$	Substring operator

ARITHMETIC OPERATORS

( )	Parentheses for grouping
/	Division
*	Multiplication

+	Addition
–	Subtraction
* * or ˆ	Exponentiation

RELATIONAL OPERATORS

<	Less than
>	Greater than
=	Equal to
<> or #	Not equal to
<=	Less than or equal to
>=	Greater than or equal to

STRING OPERATORS

+	String concatenation—trailing spaces are left intact
–	String concatenation—trailing spaces of the string preceding the operator moved to the end of the string.

FUNCTIONS

* Delete indicator; identifies record marked for deletion.

$(exp,start,length) Substring; extracts the specified part of (exp) from the given starting position for the given length.

DATE( ) Invokes name of the system variable containing the system date.

EOF End-of-file function; evaluates as a logical true/false whether the last record of the file in use has been processed.

STR(exp,length,decimals) String function; converts the specified portion of (exp) to a character string.

TRIM(exp) Trim function; removes trailing blanks from a specified string variable.

? Displays the value of an expression to the output device.

@ Used with a Get or Say command to specify the row and column of output.

SELECTED dBASE COMMANDS

ACCEPT <'prompt'> TO <memvar> In command files, assumes that the data are string and places them in the designated memory variable specified by the To parameter.

APPEND [BLANK] Adds record(s) or blank formatted record(s) to the database file in use.

APPEND FROM <file> Appends data from a database.

ASSIST Activates the Control Center.

AVERAGE <explist> [WHILE <condition>] [FOR <condition>] Calculates the arithmetic average for numeric fields.

BROWSE [FIELDS <field list>] Provides full-screen editing for changing a file.

CLEAR Erases the screen.

CLEAR ALL Closes all database files, index files, format files, and relations; releases all memory variables and selects work area one.

CLOSE ALL   Closes all files of all types and reselects work area.

COMPILE <filename> [runtime]   Reads a file containing dBASE IV source code and creates an executable object code file.

CONTINUE   Continues a Locate command.

COPY TO <file> [FIELD <list>]   Copies the file or fields from the file in use to the designated database file.

COPY TO <file> STRUCTURE [FIELD <list>]   Copies the structure of the file in use to the designated file.

COUNT [<scope>] [FOR/WHILE <condition>] [TO <memvar>]   Counts the number of records in the database that match the specified condition; if a memory variable has been specified, places the result there.

CREATE LABEL <.lbl filename>   Activates the Label menu and lets you create a label form file.

CREATE QUERY <.qry filename>   Activates the Query menu and lets you create a filter condition and store it to a .QRY file.

CREATE REPORT <.frm filename>   Activates the Report menu and lets you create a report template and store it to a .FRM file.

CREATE SCREEN <.scr filename>   Activates the Screen menu and lets you create a custom screen format and store it to a .SCR file.

CREATE STRUCTURE [<file>]   Starts the creation process for a database file.

DELETE [<scope>] [FOR <exp>]   Marks record(s) for deletion.

DELETE FILE <file>   Deletes the specified file.

DIR [<drive>] [<path>]   Shows the files on the specified drive or path.

DISPLAY [<scope>] [<field list>] [FOR <exp>] [OFF]   Displays selected records from the database file in use.

DISPLAY MEMORY   Displays current memory variables.

DISPLAY STATUS   Displays current information about active databases, index files, alternate files, and system parameters.

DISPLAY STRUCTURE   Displays the structure of the file in use.

DO <.prg filename>   Executes a program file.

DO CASE   Used in place of a nested If command when multiple conditions must be tested. (Each Case contains a condition to be tested. The Otherwise command traps a transaction that has not met any of the specified conditions. There must be a corresponding Endcase command to denote the end of the range of the Do Case.)

DO WHILE <condition>   Executes the program statements through the Enddo until the condition specified in the Do While has been met.

EDIT [n]   Starts selective editing of the file in use.

EJECT PAGE   Sends a form feed to the printer.

ERASE <filename>   Deletes the specified file from the directory.

FIND <character string>   Positions the record pointer to the first record with an index key that matches the specified character string, which does not have to be delimited.

GO or GOTO <n> or TOP, or <BOTTOM>   Positions the pointer at a specific record or place in the file in use.

HELP [<dBASE IV keyword>]   Menu-driven help feature that provides information about dBASE.

IF <condition>   The If statement allows a condition to be evaluated and,
    <statements>   if the condition is true, for the statements before the Else
ELSE   to be executed. Otherwise, the conditions following the
    <statements>   Else are executed.
ENDIF

GET   Obtains data from a user via interactive input from the keyboard. (A corresponding Picture is often used to specify the format and type of character that can be entered.)

IMPORT FROM <filename> [TYPE] PFS / dBASE II / FW2 / RPD / WK1   Creates a dBASE file from these file types.

INDEX ON <key> TAG   Creates an index for the file in use.

INPUT <'prompt'> TO <memvar>   In command files, assumes that the data are numeric, unless enclosed in quotes, and places them in the memory variable specified by the To parameter.

INSERT [BEFORE] [BLANK]   Inserts a record into the database; if the Before parameter is used, places the record before the current record; if the Blank parameter is not used, invokes EDIT mode for the new record.

LABEL FORM <.lbl filename> [WHILE <condition>] [FOR<condition>] [TO PRINT]   Prints labels using the indicated label form file.

LIST [<scope>] [<field list>] [FOR <exp>] [OFF]   Lists records from the file in use.

LIST FILES [ON <disk drive>] [LIKE <skeleton>]   Lists files from disk.

LIST STRUCTURE   Displays the structure of the file in use.

LOCATE [<scope>] [FOR <exp>]   Finds the first record that satisfies the specified condition; the Continue command is then used to locate the next record meeting the condition.

MODIFY COMMAND <file>   Calls dBASE text editor and brings up the designated file for modification.

MODIFY LABEL <filename>   Activates the Label menu for changing .LBL file parameters.

MODIFY QUERY <filename>   Activates the Query menu for changing .QRY file parameters.

MODIFY REPORT <filename>   Activates the Report menu for changing .FRM report template parameters.

MODIFY SCREEN <filename>   Activates the Screen menu for changing .SCR file parameters.

MODIFY STRUCTURE   Allows structural modification of a database file.

PACK   Eliminates records marked for deletion.

PICTURE   Used with a Say or Get command, controls how data will be printed or displayed to the screen; allowable picture template characters: $, #, *, 9, commas, and decimal points.

QUIT   Terminates dBASE and returns control to the operating system.

READ   In command files, makes the values obtained by Get available to the program for processing.

RECALL [<scope>] [FOR <exp>]   Recovers records previously marked for deletion.

REINDEX   Rebuilds existing active index files.

RENAME <oldfile> TO <newfile>   Lets you rename a file.

REPLACE [<scope>] <field> WITH <exp> [FOR <exp>]   Replaces the value of the specified field of specified records with stated values.

REPORT [FORM <filename>] [<scope>] [FOR <exp>] [TO PRINT]   Generates or accesses an existing .FRM file for output of data in a defined format.

RETURN   Returns control to calling program, to the Control Center, or to the dot prompt.

SEEK <expression>   Positions the record pointer to the first record with an index key that matches the specified expression.

SELECT <work area/alias>   Activates the specified work area for accessing a file.

SET   See SET commands.

SKIP [+ − n]   Moves the pointer forward or backward within the file.

SORT ON <key> TO <file> [ASCENDING] or [DESCENDING]   Creates another database file, sorted in the order specified by the named key.

SORT TO <new filename> ON <field list> [/A] [C] [/D]   Creates an ordered copy of a database, arranged according to one or more fields.

STORE <expression> TO <memvar>   Stores the results of the expression in the designated memory variable.

SUM <field list> [TO <memvar list>] [<scope>] [FOR <exp>]   Computes and displays the sum of numeric fields.

TYPE <filename> [TO PRINT]   Displays the contents of a file; To Print parameter dumps a copy of the file to the printer.

UPDATE ON <key> FROM <alias> REPLACE <field> WITH <expression> RANDOM   Provides for a batch update of a presorted or indexed file.

USE <file> [INDEX <file list>]   Opens a database file and (optionally) opens desired index files.

WAIT <'prompt'> TO <memvar>   In command files, places the single character of data entered from the keyboard in the memory variable specified by the To parameter as soon as Enter is pressed; if no <'prompt'> is included, displays the message Press any key to continue....

ZAP   Removes all records from the active database file.

SELECTED SET COMMANDS

Set commands let you redefine the environment in which you are working with dBASE. The default value of each Set command of On/Off type is indicated by the order of presentation: Off/On indicates that the default is off; On/Off indicates that the default is on.

SET ALTERNATE OFF   Stops the echoing of output to the specified .TXT file and closes the file.

SET ALTERNATE ON   In conjunction with a Set Alternate To command, starts the echoing of output to the specified .TXT file.

SET ALTERNATE TO <filename>   Specifies the .TXT file that is to receive the echoed output to the screen (the .TXT contains standard ASCII output) and closes any currently open Alternate files. You can also close an alternate file via the command Close Alternate.

SET BELL ON/OFF   On rings the bell when invalid data are entered or a field boundary is passed; Off turns off the bell.

SET CONFIRM OFF/ON   Does not skip to the next field in the full-screen mode.

SET CONSOLE ON/OFF   Turns the screen display on and off from within the program.

SET DATE TO <MM/DD/YY>   Sets or resets the system date.

SET DECIMALS TO <expN>   Sets the minimum number of decimals displayed in the results of certain operations and functions.

SET DEFAULT TO <drive>   Commands dBASE IV to regard the specified drive as the default drive for all future operations.

SET DELETED OFF/ON   On prevents dBASE IV from reading/processing any record marked for deletion following a command that has <scope>; Off allows dBASE IV to read all records.

SET DEVICE TO PRINT/SCREEN   Determines where @Say commands will be routed.

SET EXACT ON   Results in only those records being found whose characters exactly meet the criteria used in a Seek command.

SET FILTER TO [FILE <.qry filename>]   Causes a database file to appear to contain only records that meet the specified condition.

SET HEADINGS ON/OFF   Determines whether column titles are shown above each field for DISPLAY, LIST, SUM, and AVERAGE.

SET INTENSITY ON/OFF   On enables inverse video or dual intensity to appear during full-screen operations; Off disables these features.

SET MARGIN TO <n>   Sets the left-hand margin of the printer to <n>.

SET MENU ON/OFF   Turns menus on or off.

SET VIEW TO <query filename>   Performs a query as specified (.QBE or .QBO) in a query file.

FULL-SCREEN CURSOR MOVEMENT CODES

ALL COMMANDS

Ctrl + Right Arrow or Ctrl + X   Moves the cursor down to the next field (also Ctrl + F).

Up Arrow or Ctrl + E   Moves cursor up to the previous field (also Ctrl + A).

Right Arrow or Ctrl + D   Moves cursor ahead one character.

Left Arrow or Ctrl + S   Moves cursor back one character.

Del or Ctrl + G   Deletes character under cursor.

Backspace   Deletes character to the left of cursor.

Ctrl + Y   Blanks out current field to right of cursor.

Ins or Ctrl + V   Toggles between OVERWRITE and INSERT modes.

Ctrl + End or Ctrl + W   Saves changes and returns to command (.) prompt.

IN EDIT MODE

Ctrl + U   Toggles the record delete mark on and off.

Pg Dn or Ctrl + C   Writes current record to disk and advances to next record.

Pg Up or Ctrl + R   Writes current record to disk and backs to previous record.

Esc   Ignores changes to current record and returns to command (.) prompt.

Ctrl + End or Ctrl + W   Writes all changes to disk and returns to command (.) prompt.

IN BROWSE MODE

Tab   Pans the window right one field.

Shift + Tab   Pans the window left one field.

IN MODIFY MODE

Ctrl + T   Deletes current line and moves all lower lines up.

Ctrl + N   Inserts new line at cursor position.

Ctrl + C   Scrolls down one-half page.

Ctrl + End or Ctrl + W   Writes all changes onto disk and returns to command (.) prompt.

Esc   Ignores all changes and returns to Assist or dot prompt.

IN APPEND MODE

Enter   Terminates Append when cursor is in first position of first field.

Ctrl + End or Ctrl + W   Writes record to disk and moves to next record.

Esc   Ignores current record and returns to command (.) prompt.

GLOSSARY

A> (DOS prompt): The message to the user that indicates the default disk and that DOS is ready to receive a message.

acronym: Word formed from letters or syllables in a name or phrase. For example, FORTRAN is an acronym for FORmula TRANslator.

active directory: The active directory on a disk device is the last directory that you were in via a CD command. Any files copied to the disk name (with no path specified) get copied to this directory.

active index: The index that dBASE uses to locate records within a file.

address: (As a noun) number associated with each memory location; (as a verb) to refer to a particular memory location.

All parameter: The dBASE scope parameter that includes all records of a file in a command.

alphanumeric: Combination of the words *alphabetic* and *numeric*. A set of alphanumeric characters usually includes special characters such as the dollar sign and comma.

alphanumeric keys: Keys that contain a letter of the alphabet, a number, or a special character.

Alt: Key label for the Alternate key.

Alternate key: Key used for the following purposes: to create a second set of function keys in some application programs, to enter the ASCII character code directly from the keyboard, and (together with letters) to enter BASIC commands.

ANSI.SYS (file): A file that DOS uses to enter, output, and report data (characters).

application program: Precoded set of generalized instructions for the computer, written to accomplish a certain goal. Examples of such programs include a general ledger package, a mailing list program, and PacMan.

Arrow keys: Keys (Down, Up, Right, and Left) found on the numeric keyboard and typically used to move a pointer or cursor.

ASCII: Acronym for American Standard Code for Information Interchange (pronounced *ass-key*). Often called USASCII, this code is a standard method of representing a character with a number inside the computer. Knowledge of the code is important only if you write programs.

AUTOEXEC.BAT: File that is executed by the computer as soon as the boot process is completed. This type of file is used in building a turnkey application that requires very little input from a user before starting.

Average command: The dBASE command that calculates the average for all records containing the specified field.

Backspace key: Key used to erase the last character typed. It is labeled with an arrow that points toward the left.

batch file: A file with a .BAT extension that holds DOS commands and can be executed.

beginning-of-file (BOF) command: dBASE command that checks to determine if the beginning of the file has been reached.

bell: Sound produced by your computer or line printer, often used by programs to get your attention or to reassure you that computer processing is underway.

binary: Number system consisting of two digits, 0 and 1, with each digit in a binary number representing a power of 2. Most digital computers are binary. A binary signal is easily expressed by the presence or absence of an electrical current or magnetic field.

bit: Binary digit, the smallest amount of information a computer can hold. A single bit specifies a single value of 0 or 1. Bits can be grouped to form larger values (see *byte* and *nibble*).

boot process: Process of starting the computer. During the boot process, a memory check is performed, the various parts of DOS are loaded, and the date and time are requested.

boot record: Record that resides on sector 0 of track 0 of a disk and contains the program responsible for loading the rest of DOS into the microcomputer.

Bottom: dBASE command that enables you to position the pointer at the end of the file.

bottom margin: The amount of blank space at the bottom of each page.

Browse: dBASE command that displays a number of records on the screen at one time, letting you edit a file quickly.

BUFFERS: The DOS command that lets you determine how much RAM is used for holding information for disk read/write operations. This command is used in the CONFIG.SYS file.

bug: Error. A hardware bug is a physical or electrical malfunction or design error; a software bug is an error in programming, either in the logic of the program or in typing.

bus: Entity that enables the computer to pass information to a peripheral and to receive information from a peripheral.

byte: Basic unit of measure of a computer's memory. A byte usually has eight bits, and therefore its value can be from 0 to 255. Each character can be represented by one byte in ASCII.

Caps Lock key: Key used to switch the case of letters A through Z on the keyboard. This key does not affect numbers and special characters.

card: General term for a printed circuit board with electronic components attached. It is also called an interface card, a board, a circuit card assembly, and other similar names.

Cathode-ray tube: See *CRT.*

centering hole: Large hole on a diskette that allows the Mylar plastic disk inside the diskette envelope to center on the capstan for proper rotation.

central processing unit (CPU): Device in a computer system that contains the arithmetic unit, the control unit, and the main memory. It is also referred to as the computer.

character: Any graphic symbol that has a specific meaning to people. Letters (both upper- and lowercase), numbers, and various symbols (such as punctuation marks) are all characters.

character field: Field capable of holding any alphanumeric or special character. In dBASE, such a field can hold up to 254 characters.

chip: Electronic entity containing one or more semiconductors on a wafer of silicon, within which an integrated circuit is formed.

clock speed: The speed, in megahertz, used to control how fast the operations within a computer are performed.

closed-bus system: Type of computer system that comes with plugs, called established ports, that accept device cables from the peripheral.

COBOL: Acronym for Common Business-Oriented Language, a high-level language oriented toward organizational data-processing procedures.

code: Method of representing something in terms of something else. The ASCII code represents characters in terms of binary numbers; the BASIC language represents algorithms in terms of program statements. *Code* may also refer to programs, usually in low-level languages.

cold start: Boot process used to begin operating a computer that has just been turned on.

color monitor: Display device that is capable of showing red, green, and blue colors.

column: Vertical line of text.

COMMAND.COM: Command processor of DOS, containing built-in functions or subroutines that let you copy a file or get a directory listing of a disk.

common field: A field that has the same name and contents and appears in more than one file.

compiler: Software that translates a program into machine language. As it performs this translation, it also checks for errors made by the programmer.

computer: Any device that can receive and store a set of instructions and then act on those instructions in a predetermined and predictable fashion. The definition implies that both the instructions and the data on which the instructions act can be changed; a device whose instructions cannot be changed is not a computer.

concatenation: Process of joining two character strings, usually accomplished through the use of the + sign.

CONFIG.SYS: The file used by DOS after the boot process is finished to further configure your computer system.

configured software: Software that has been customized to the specific hardware configuration currently used.

constant data: Information that remains the same from one document to the next.

Continue: dBASE command that finds the next record in a Locate command search.

control key: General-purpose key whose uses include invoking breaks, pauses, system resets, clear screens, print echos, and various edit commands. In instructions, the Control key is often represented as a caret (^).

coprocessor: Microprocessor chip that is placed in a microcomputer to take the burden of manipulating numbers off the CPU, allowing it to perform other tasks.

COPY: DOS and dBASE (Copy) command that copies one or more files onto the current disk or onto another disk. In spreadsheets, it enables you to copy the contents of a cell into one or more other cells; in WordPerfect (Copy), it lets you copy a block of text to another location in a document.

Copy Field command: dBASE command that lets you copy the contents of a field(s) and create a separate file.

Copy Structure command: dBASE command that creates an empty file with the fields from the sending file.

CPU: See *Central processing unit.*

Create: dBASE command that lets you build a database and describe the fields and the data type of each field.

Create Report command: dBASE command that lets you create a report template containing the settings to be used in generating a printed report.

CRT: An abbreviation for *cathode ray tube,* meaning any television screen or device containing such a screen.

Ctrl: Key label for the Control key.

cursor control key: One of the four Arrow keys on the numeric keypad used to move the cursor left, right, up, or down on the screen.

cursor movement: Operation of moving the cursor over the text.

data (datum): Information of any kind.

database: Collection of data related to one specific type of application. *Database* is often used synonymously with *file.*

database management: The ability to input, store, report, and manipulate data.

DATE: DOS command that lets you change the system date.

dBASE II: Relational database package.

dBASE III: Updated version of dBASE II.

dBASE III Plus: The updated version of dBASE III.

dBASE IV (Release 1.1): The latest version of dBASE.

debug: To find hardware or software faults and eliminate them.

default: Original (or initial) setting of a software package.

default disk drive: Disk drive that is accessed automatically by the microcomputer when a file-oriented command is executed.

Del: Key label for the Delete key.

Delete: dBASE command that lets you mark a record for later deletion. The term *delete* also refers to the ability of a word processing package to remove text from a document.

Delete File command: dBASE command that lets you delete a file contained on disk.

delete indicator: Asterisk (*) that appears in a record when it has been marked for deletion.

Delete key: Key used to erase the character to the left of the current cursor position.

Delimited parameter: dBASE command that lets you place specific characters around fields that are to be copied.

delimiter: Character that indicates to the computer where one part of a command ends and another part begins. Typical delimiters are the space, the period, and the comma.

DIR: DOS command that is used to list the files in the directory.

directory: Part of a diskette that holds the names of files stored on it. The directory also contains information about file size, file extensions, the files' location on diskette, and the dates and times the files were created or changed.

Directory (DIR) command: dBASE command that lets you list specified files from disk.

directory (subdirectory): Like a root directory except that it is itself a file and contains DOS housekeeping entries in a regular directory; it does not have the size limitation of the root directory.

disk drive: Rectangular box, connected to or situated inside the computer, that reads and writes into diskettes.

diskette: Square recordlike objects used for storing information from the computer. (Also called a disk or floppy disk.)

Disk operating system: See *DOS*.

display: (As a noun) any sort of output device for a computer, usually a video screen; (as a verb) to place information on such a screen.

Display command: dBASE command that displays the record at the pointer location.

DOS: Acronym for Disk Operating System, the program responsible for letting you interact with the many parts of a computer system. DOS (pronounced *doss*) is the interface between you and the hardware. To perform system functions, DOS commands are typed on the keyboard, but DOS is actually a collection of programs designed to make it easy to create and manage files, run programs, and use system devices attached to the computer.

dot-matrix printer: Printer that generates characters by firing seven or nine tiny print heads against a ribbon.

double-density disks: Disks that have approximately twice the storage of a single-density disk. This is achieved by using a higher-quality read/write surface on the disk, so that data can be stored in a denser format.

double-sided disks: Disks on which data can be stored on both surfaces. A double-sided disk has been certified (tested) on both sides.

edit: Process by which the format of data is modified for output by inserting dollar signs, blanks, and so on. Used as a verb, to validate and rearrange input data.

EGA monitor: Abbreviation for enhanced graphics adapter. A video device that is capable of presenting clear, vivid graphics. It uses a 640 x 350 (or more) dot resolution to present crisper, more colorful images.

End key: Key used together with the Ctrl key to erase characters on the screen from the current cursor position to the end of the line.

end-of-file (EOF) command: dBASE command that checks to determine if the end of the file has been reached.

Enter/Return key: The key that is pressed to indicate that you have finished entering an instruction or a paragraph.

error message: Message informing you that you did not type something the program can process or that some other system failure has occurred.

Esc: Key label for the Escape key.

Escape key: Key used for general purposes, usually to cause some change in computer processing. In DOS and BASIC, it is used to erase a line of input; in application programs, it is often used to transfer to another section of the program.

execute: To perform the intent of a command or instruction; to run a program or a portion of a program.

expansion board: Printed circuit board that can be inserted into an open-bus expansion slot, expanding the computer configuration to include such items as modems and plotters.

extension: One- to three-character portion of a filename. Extensions are typically used to indicate families of files, such as backups (.BK!), regular database files (.DBF), and indexes (.NDX).

field: Subdivision of a record that holds one piece of data about a transaction.

file: Collection of data or programs that serves a single purpose. A file is stored on a diskette and given a name so that you can recall it.

filename: Unique identifier of a file, composed of one to eight characters. If an optional one- to three-character extension is used, there must be a period between the filename and the filename extension.

filename extension: The three-character portion of a filename that lets you create families of files. If used, a period must be included.

Find: dBASE command used to locate records in an indexed file, using the index.

For parameter: dBASE command that lets you specify which records are to be included in a command.

functions: Formulas or processes built into a software package. These functions save a user a tremendous amount of effort and tedium.

Goto: dBASE command used to position the pointer at a specific record in a file.

Goto Bottom command: dBASE command that positions the pointer at the last record.

Goto Top command: dBASE command that positions the pointer at the first record.

hard copy: Printed document on paper.

hard disk: Rigid medium for storing computer information, usually rated in megabytes (millions of bytes) of storage capacity.

hardware: Physical parts of a computer.

Index: dBASE command used to order information logically within a file without physically reordering the records themselves. Indexes may be single- or multiple-field.

initialization: Process during the boot routine when the computer activates the various peripherals hooked to the computer.

Ins: Key label for the Insert key.

Insert key: Key used to tell the computer program that you want to insert characters to the left of the cursor. The INSERT mode continues until you press the key again or until you press another special key (cursor arrows, Del, End) indicating that you want to go on to a different editing operation.

instruction: Smallest portion of a program that a computer can execute.

interpreter: Program, usually written in machine language, that understands and executes a higher-level language one statement at a time.

K: Abbreviation for the Greek prefix *kilo-*, meaning *thousand*. In computer-related usage, K usually represents the quantity 2^{10}, or 1,024.

key: Data item (field) that identifies a record.

keyboard: System hardware used to input characters, commands, and functions to the computer. The keyboard consists of 83 keys and is organized into three sections: the function keys, the typewriter keyboard, and the numeric keypad.

language: Code that both the programmer and the computer understand. The programmer uses the language to express what is to be done, and the computer understands the language and performs the desired actions.

language processor: Software that translates a high-level language such as COBOL or BASIC into machine-understandable code.

List: dBASE command used to display records from a data file contained on disk.

List Files Like command: dBASE command that lets you list files containing a specific extension.

List structure: Structure arrangement containing records that are linked together by pointers.

List Structure command: dBASE command that displays the file's record structure to the screen.

Locate: dBASE command used to find data in a sequential file.

Lock key: Key used to cause subsequent key operations to be interpreted in a specific manner by the computer. Lock keys are toggle keys; they include Caps, Num, and Scroll.

logical field: Field capable of holding the values of .T. (true) or .F. (false) or Y (yes) or N (no). Logical fields are always 1-byte fields.

logical operator: The dBASE operators .AND., .OR., and .NOT..

machine language: Lowest-level language. Machine language is usually binary; instructions in machine language are single-byte opcodes, sometimes followed by various operands.

Megabyte (MB,M): One million characters of storage, a quantity usually used as a measure of available storage on a hard disk.

memory location: Smallest subdivision of the memory map to which the computer can refer. Each memory location has a unique address and a certain value.

menu: List of commands available to anyone using a software package.

microcomputer: Computer based on a microprocessor (8-bit, 16-bit, or 32-bit) that can execute a single user's program.

microcomputer system: Combined computer, disk drives, monitor, and input and output devices for data processing.

microprocessor: Integrated circuit that understands and executes machine-language programs.

mixed-data index: An index that contains both character and numeric data. The numeric data must be converted to characters when building the index.

Modify Command command: dBASE command that invokes the dBASE editor.

MS DOS: Operating system developed by Microsoft. It is the same as PC DOS except that there is no ROM BASIC provision. This operating system is used by most IBM-compatible computers.

multiple-field index: An index that is created by concatenating two fields of data.

nested function: Function that resides inside another function. The innermost function must be executed before any outer ones.

Next command: dBASE command that moves the pointer forward or backward in a file.

NO FIND message: The message displayed by dBASE if it is unable to find a record in a SEEK or FIND command.

numeric data: Data consisting of the digits 0 through 9.

numeric entry: Process of entering numbers into the computer. The numeric keypad can be set into numeric entry mode via the Num Lock key; after this has been done, numbers and number symbols (decimal, minus, plus) can be entered.

numeric field: Field that can hold only a number or a decimal point. No alphabetic or special characters can be placed in such a field.

numeric key pad: Section of the keyboard containing numeric entry and editing keys.

Numeric Lock key: Key used to switch the numeric keypad back and forth between numeric entry and editing.

Num Lock: Key label for the Numeric Lock key.

object code: Machine-language code created by the compiler. It is the object code that is actually executed by the computer.

output: Computer-generated data whose destination is the screen, disk, printer, or some other output device.

Pack: dBASE command that physically removes any records marked for deletion.

Page Down key: Key that is sometimes used to cause text on the screen to move down. Text on the bottom of the screen moves offscreen while text is added at the top.

Page Up key: Key that is sometimes used to cause text on the screen to move up. Text on the top of the screen moves offscreen while text is added at the bottom.

parameter: Modifying piece of information that constitutes part of a DOS or dBASE command. It might, for example, indicate which files or fields are to be included in an operation.

pause: Computer function that can be used at any time to temporarily halt the program in use. Pause is invoked by pressing the Num Lock key while holding down the Ctrl key. Pressing any key after a Pause causes the computer to continue from the point of interruption. Pause can also be performed with one hand by pressing the key combination Ctrl + S.

Pg Dn: Key label for the Page Down key.

Pg Up: Key label for the Page Up key.

precedence: Order in which calculations are executed.

Press any key to continue: Message often displayed by a program when the computer is waiting for you to do something (read text or load a diskette, for example) and does not know when you will be done. Some keys are generally inactive and do not cause the program to continue when they are pressed; these include the Alt, Shift, Ctrl, Scroll Lock, Num Lock, and Caps Lock keys.

primary key: In dBASE, the record number; in sorting, the major sort field.

primary memory: Internal memory used by the computer for a number of different functions. It can contain data, program instructions, or intermediate results of calculations.

printer: Device used to make a permanent copy of any output.

procedures: Written instructions on how to use hardware or software.

query: The process of asking a question and obtaining a response from a database.

? command: dBASE command that displays the result of a function or command to the default output device (screen or printer).

Quit: dBASE command that returns you to the operating system.

random-access memory (RAM): Main memory of a computer. The acronym RAM can be used to refer either to the integrated circuits that make up this type of memory or to the memory itself. The computer can store values in distinct locations in RAM and then recall them, or it can alter and restore them.

read-only memory (ROM): Memory usually used to hold important programs or data that must be available to the computer when power is first turned on. Information in ROM is placed there during the process of manufacture and is unalterable. Information stored in ROM does not disappear when power is turned off.

Recall: dBASE command used to retrieve or unmark records that have been marked for deletion.

Recall All command: dBASE command that undeletes any record that was marked for deletion.

record: Entity that contains information about a specific business happening or transaction.

record number: Identification used by dBASE as the primary key for a record; the physical location in the file for a given record.

relational structure: Structural arrangement consisting of one or more tables. Data are stored in the form of relations in these tables.

Report: dBASE command that creates or accesses a parameter file, modifying how a specific printed report is to be generated.

Report Form command: dBASE command that generates a report using a report template.

report template: A dBASE .FRM file that contains all the commands which are necessary for a report to be generated.

scroll: Function that moves all the text on a display (usually upward) to make room for more (usually at the bottom).

Shift key: Key used to select the uppercase character on keys that have two characters or to reverse the case of letters *A* through *Z*, depending on the status of the Caps Lock key.

single-field index: An index created by dBASE using the contents of a single field.

Skip: dBASE command used to move the pointer forward or backward within a data file.

skip sequential processing: The process of moving to a record via a FIND or SEEK command and then processing the records sequentially from that point.

SORT: DOS filter command used to store data files; also the dBASE (Sort) command used to reorder a database file physically.

source code: Set of program instructions written in a high-level language.

source drive: Drive that contains any files which are to be copied.

source file: A file that contains data that are to be linked to a target file in a 1-2-3 file link operation.

storage: Term that applies to either RAM or external disk memory.

STR (string) function: dBASE command that changes numeric data to character.

subroutine: Segment of a program that can be executed by a single call. Subroutines perform the same sequence of instructions at many different places in a single program.

Substring function ($): dBASE command that locates a character string anywhere within a record field.

Sum: dBASE command used to total the contents of a field for all records within a file.

syntax: Structure of instructions in a language. If you make a mistake in entering an instruction and garble the syntax, the computer sometimes responds with the message SYNTAX ERROR.

system reset: System function that restarts your computer just like a power on/off. This is accomplished by pressing Del while holding down Ctrl and Alt. Three keys are required to ensure that you know what you are doing and to avoid an accidental system reset.

target drive: Disk to which files will be copied.

testing: Process by which a program or worksheet is examined and tried out to make certain that it generates the proper results.

text characters: Letters and numbers, usually in English.

toggle key: Key with two states, ON and OFF, that causes subsequent key operations to be processed in a predetermined manner. Toggle keys include the Caps Lock, Num Lock, and Scroll Lock keys.

Top: dBASE command used to position the pointer at the beginning of a data file.

To Printer option: dBASE command that prints the output of a List or Report Form command.

Trim function: dBASE command that lets you delete lower-order blanks from a field.

typewriter keyboard: One of the three main key groupings of a computer system keyboard. It contains the QWERTY typewriter keyboard, as well as some special keys such as Enter, Backspace, Tab, Esc, and Alt.

Update command: dBASE command that lets you use the contents of one file to update another file.

upper case: Set of upper characters on two-character keys and capital letters (*A* to *Z*). Any uppercase character can be typed by holding down the Shift key while pressing the desired key.

Use command: The dBASE command that makes a file available for manipulation.

View command: Lotus command that generates a graph on the screen. Also, the dBASE command that displays fields from one or more files at a time.

volatile memory: Memory that is erased when the electrical current to the computer is turned off.

warm start: Booting process used to restart a computer after you have lost control of its language or operating system.

write-protected: Diskettes protected from: having information stored on them, being altered, or being deleted; this is accomplished by placing a write-protect tab over the small rectangular hole on the side of a diskette.

INDEX

dBASE

File Commands

Create	Append	Use
Delete File	Edit	Modify
Copy File	Browse	Pack
Display Structure	Index	

Pointer

GOTO #
Skip
Find
Locate

Operators

Logical	Arithmetic	Relational	
.OR.	+ Addition	< Less than	<= Less than or equal
.AND.	– Subtraction	> Greater than	>= Greater than or equal
.NOT.	* Multiplication	= Equal	
	/ Division	<> Not equal	

---

dBASE

Selected Set Commands

Set Bell On/Off — On rings the bell when invalid data are entered or a field boundary is passed. Off turns off the bell.

Set Colon On/Off — On displays colons which delimit or bound input fields: Off hides the colons. (Only dBASE II)

Set Default to ⟨drive⟩ — Commands dBASE to regard the specified drive as the default drive for all future operations.

Set Deleted Off/On — On prevents dBASE from reading/processing any record marked for deletion. Off allows dBASE to read all records.

Set Intensity On/Off — On enables inverse video or dual intensity during full-screen operations. Off disables these features.

Set Margin to ⟨n⟩ — Sets the lefthand margin of printer to ⟨n⟩.

---

dBASE

Selected Full-Screen Cursor Movement Commands

^X	Moves DOWN to next field	⟨DEL⟩	Deletes character to left of cursor
^E	Moves UP to next field	^Y	Blanks out current field
^D	Moves RIGHT one position	^V	Toggle between overwrite and insert mode
^S	Moves LEFT one position	^W	Save changes and return to "." prompt
^G	Deletes character at cursor		

Other Common Commands

ESC	Cancel any command and return to "." prompt
^Q	Ignore any changes and return to "." prompt
^N	Insert a line at cursor's position (Modify)
^T	Delete current line and move text up (Modify)
^P	Toggle printer On/Off